12/04

To Minch

Keep on Cooking!

tyler florence's real kitchen

tyler florence's real kitchen

Text with JoAnn Cianciulli
Photographs by Bill Bettencourt

 Clarkson Potter/Publishers New York

Published by Clarkson Potter/Publishers, New York, New York.
Member of the Crown Publishing Group, a division of Random House, Inc.
www.randomhouse.com

CLARKSON N. POTTER is a trademark and POTTER and colophon are registered trademarks of Random House, Inc.

Printed in China

Design by Subtitle - NYC

Library of Congress Cataloging-in-Publication Data
Florence, Tyler.
Tyler Florence's real kitchen / by Tyler Florence; photographs by Bill Bettencourt;
foreword by Bobby Flay.
Includes index.
1. Cookery. I. Title.
TX714 .F637   2003
641.5—dc21   2002012279

ISBN 0-609-60997-1

10   9   8   7   6

Thanks

I am incredibly proud of this project. If you've never had the experience of putting a cookbook together (and I didn't), know that it is a monster of a task. *Real Kitchen* took two years write, test, shoot, and edit, and by no means did I do it alone. Some days were inspiring, and I burned through pages with lighting speed; other days I would have preferred root canal surgery to retesting the same recipe for the umpteenth time. But at the end of it all, I wouldn't change a minute of the process. Through it, I am a better cook today.

The adage that you are only as good as the people around you is so true. Without the small band of renegades that helped, coached, and consulted on this book, this project would have looked like a second grade book report written by a monkey on an Etch-a Sketch. My thanks go to:

Evyn Block, my girlfriend and life editor, for putting up with me, loving me, and always having a good idea; JoAnn Cianciulli, the other woman in my life, producer, and lifelong friend. Without your dedication, organization, and planning this book would not have happened. I can't thank you enough.

Bill Bettencourt, the best damn photographer in the business. You brought the book to a whole different level. Thank you and congrats on your beautiful baby daughter.

Corinne Alhadeff, for testing the recipes down to a grain of salt. They're all perfect and you and David are a lot of laughs.

Pam Krauss, my editor at Clarkson Potter. It's funny how life puts two people together. Thanks for encouragement, tough love, and spell checking, and here's to a long relationship together. I also appreciate the great support I received from Amy Boorstein, Leigh Ann Ambrosi, Joan Denman, Adina Steiman, and Jane Treuhaft, all at Potter;

Bobby Flay: Thanks for clueing me in to what's what from day one. You are a great professional mentor and as sharp as they come, my friend;

The team at Subtitle for their artistic vision;

And Eileen Opatut and everyone at Food Network.

I'm also indebted to the following: My family (thanks for the support); my favorite Brooklyn provisioners, including Fish Tales and Staubitz Meat Market on Court Street, Mike and Michael at Charcuterie (thanks for all the free coffee) and Natural Land and Natural Sea, on Flatbush Avenue; Leslie Booker, "stylist to the stars"; Teresa Fox, Johannes Sanzin, and Dominique Drevet at Bistro St. Marks; Anna Weinberg, Paul Masters, Joey Cappicino, Greg and Christine Okshetyn, Andrei Petrov, Lauren Bergman, Alex Grant, Max "the love shack" Mackenzie, the Union Square Greenmarket, and Frankie "don't make me tell you the Brunello story" DeCarlo.

contents*

Foreword

I first met Tyler Florence when he was the chef at the trendy New York City eatery Cafeteria. He impressed me as a talented cook with a great passion for good food. Since then, Tyler has gone on to become one of my Food Network colleagues and the host of *Food 911,* where he has been putting out fires in home kitchens around the country and elevating the level of home cooking everywhere in the process.

Cooking at home is on the rise and with good reason—what could be more satisfying than making a dish for friends or family and having them be totally blown away? That's the kind of food you'll find in this book. Tyler doesn't focus on one style of cuisine; he's a fan of things that taste good whether they are American classics, Italian dishes both new and old, or the Asian flavors that have swept the country like a tornado. Need an excuse to weed out your pantry and toss those tired old spices? Tyler will help you stock your shelves so you're ready for almost anything. Think how diversified your pantry will be with Asian ingredients like Chinese black vinegar, sesame oil, Latin chile peppers, and Italian products like Arborio rice and polenta.

This is food anyone—even a chef—needs in his repertoire. I know which ones I'll be making first. When was the last time you had a great Chicken Cacciatore, a dish that makes the whole neighborhood smell good, with roasted peppers and tomatoes, with that cutting natural saltiness of capers and anchovies (a great place to sneak in the anchovies on your friends). Thick Pork Chops with Spiced Apples and Raisins reminds me of my childhood, and I know my mother would be happy with this rendition. And what's better than Cold Fried Chicken? This is the first time I have come across a recipe that actually suggests frying the chicken and letting it chill in the refrigerator—even though we all know that's why we fry chicken in the first place. (It's kind of like roasting the turkey on Thanksgiving Day so we can have sandwiches the following afternoon.) And after seeing Tyler's classic recipe for cheesecake, this New York end-of-the-meal icon will be making a return engagement to my table sooner rather than later.

Tyler's style is straightforward, savory, and smart and his recipes are always clear and concise. Use him as your guide in the kitchen and you will be happy—even your four-year-old will be content! With *Tyler Florence's Real Kitchen* in hand, you can delete the numbers "911" from your culinary speed dial.

Enjoy Tyler's cuisine. I have and I know you will, too.

Bobby Flay

Introduction

I've been cooking professionally in one capacity or another for almost fifteen years, cutting my teeth in restaurants in my home state of South Carolina and later in New York City. Working in restaurants, it was exciting having access to the priciest and most intriguing ingredients—not to mention plenty of kitchen staff to assist with the prep work and cleanup—and I loved dreaming up elaborate presentations that made my customers sit up and take notice.

So it was something of a wake-up call when I started taping my shows for Food Network. While traveling and cooking with people all over the country, I found that home cooks weren't really interested in recreating my feats of culinary virtuosity at home; in fact, they all said the same thing: Give us real food with simple ingredients that we can enjoy with family and friends. My viewers gave me the ultimate problem to solve, and I like to think that the solution is in the pages that follow.

Don't get me wrong—none of these recipes is in any way a compromise or "dumbing down" of more sophisticated food. Simple food doesn't have to be so basic that it is boring. To the contrary, it's often been my experience that many of the cleanest, best flavors are very simple ones. What I have steered clear of are those productions that start out as an exciting cooking project, and end up taking an entire day to create, leaving you with an empty wallet and a sink filled with pots. Investing that kind of time is frustrating and really takes the fun out of cooking. Cooking should be inspirational because the ingredients are fresh, the flavors are amazing, and the final result looks beautiful. The recipes I've collected here are for the kind of meals you want to have again and again, whether the number at your table is two or twenty (or two hundred!). No esoteric cooking equipment is required, although you will find a list of the cooking gadgets and investment pieces I use most on page 13. And you'll find that most of the ingredients you'll need are things you can get your hands on at any well-stocked supermarket with maybe a trip to the farm stand or gourmet store on the way.

I hope you have as much fun tearing through this cookbook as my team and I did creating it. It was a labor of love, and I enjoyed every minute of it.

All the best,

a cook's kitchen

From choosing the right equipment to my suggestions for the contents of a perfectly stocked pantry, this chapter covers everything the home cook needs to build confidence, wow dinner guests, and generally feel like a pro in the kitchen.

Creating the perfect kitchen doesn't necessarily mean a $50,000 remodeling job with expensive cabinets and marble countertops. Many of those Tuscan-inspired brick-and-tile enclaves that you see on television or in the magazines are built for people who will never even scramble an egg in their "dream kitchen." A beautiful kitchen may improve the resale value of your house, but it doesn't make you a better cook; the only thing that can make you a better cook is *cooking.* This chapter is intended to get you inspired and well versed in the basics of cooking from a chef's perspective—not an architect's. All you really need are a few quality kitchen tools, a well-stocked pantry, a little counter space, and a few good cookbooks.

The most important things to a chef are his tools, so any chapter on building a cook's kitchen has to start with a few notes on choosing solid equipment. For most people, walking around a kitchen store is like going to a video store and hunting down a movie. You're not sure what to choose, or if the movie is going to be any good. So let me make it easy for you: A good set of knives, two or three heavy-bottomed pots and skillets, a thick cutting board, plus a few other quality tools (see the list on page 13) should really cover it. I'm not a big fan of gadgets, especially those cheap knives that never need to be sharpened. More often than not, they are a waste of money. (Although I do have a vintage Ginsu knife, circa 1977, in its original wrapper. Maybe one day when I'm old and crazy I'll try to cut a car in half with it.)

One thing: Just because the list isn't long, don't think this won't be an investment—especially if you decide to buy everything at once. The old saying that a $300 pair of shoes lasts three times as long as a $100 pair is also true for kitchen equipment: A few good pieces will last a lifetime, and sometimes longer. Most higher-end kitchen equipment (like that made by All-Clad, Wüsthof, Le Creuset, or Global) comes with a lifetime replacement warranty. (That's more than you can say for a pair of expensive shoes.) In the long run, it's more economical to buy a piece that's backed by a good warranty than one you'll have to replace again and again. If you think of cookware as an investment that will last a lifetime, you will get a lifetime of pleasure out of cooking. The following is a list of kitchen equipment in different price ranges that you should not be without.

Cutlery

Early in my career, when every kitchen position was "a learning experience" (i.e., paid very little), I would often spend the lion's share of my paycheck on a single knife. A great knife was the symbol of a cook who took his calling seriously. Wüsthof knives have been part of my chef's kit for ten years. They are made of the best high-carbon steel in the world. The factory-honed edge is razor-sharp and the weight of the knife is perfectly balanced. It's a serious cook's knife, and the best thing is that the company will replace it if it breaks. For a one-time investment of about $80 (for an 8-inch chef's knife), you will probably never have to buy another knife. Global and LamsonSharp are two other brands that I recommend. Global knives are made in Japan and are relatively new on the American market. Each knife is sculpted from a single piece of steel. With their contemporary design, these knives look like razor blades, and their silver handles look great hanging from the knife rack. An 8-inch chef's knife will run around $75, a serrated bread knife around $60, and a paring knife between $25 and $30. LamsonSharp, a small company out of Shelburne Falls, Massachusetts, has been quietly producing some of the finest cutlery in the world for more than 150 years. These beautiful, handcrafted American-made knives have perfect balance, and razor edges. With their handsome rosewood handles, these knives will definitely become family heirlooms. Their price tags are comparable to Wüsthof and Global.

Cutlery Care

A magnetic knife strip that mounts to your kitchen wall is the safest and best way to care for your expensive knives. Piling sharp knives in a drawer is not only dangerous but also can warp the handcrafted blades. Wooden knife blocks trap moisture and are hard to clean; this in turn promotes bacteria. Plus the blocks take up precious counter space. I do not put my knives in the dishwasher; a quick rinse with hot water and a soapy sponge is all you need to keep them clean.

The only proper way to maintain the factory edge of a blade is by using a whetstone. If you do not have a whetstone and are not inclined to learn how to use one, find a local cutlery or knife sharpening store; just make sure they are not using an electric sharpener. Electric sharpeners wear down the metal and shorten the life of your knife—never use one at home either! A good sharpening will actually make chopping fun and run you only about $8 for a chef's knife. Depending on how much you cook, you may need to sharpen your primary knife as often as every couple of months.

To extend the life of your newly sharpened knife, I recommend using what we call in chefspeak a steel. A sharpening steel is a honing device that keeps the blade true, which means straight and aligned. Steels are made of either ceramic, magnetized steel, or diamond-impregnated steel. A few even strokes on each side of the blade right before you start working on that masterpiece salad will keep those tomatoes paper-thin.

Pots and Pans

When it comes to pots and pans, no one makes a better product than the French. I have a few heavy copper-lined sauté pans that I picked up in Paris. I'm not going to tell you how much they cost, but let's just say that I'm glad I can write those things off on my taxes. Copper is an amazing conductor of heat and the bottoms are quite thick, so they hold heat very well. But let's get real, fancy French cookware is by no means a necessity. Here's the bottom line: A heavy-bottomed 2-gallon stockpot with a lid is a must-have for stews, braises, and simmered dishes like chili. Add to that a 4-quart and a 2-quart pot (with lids) for soups and sauces, a 12-inch skillet for sautéing in large quantities, an old-fashioned cast-iron skillet, and a nonstick omelet pan for perfect eggs in the morning. If you're in the mood to splurge, Sitram from France makes a stainless steel line that is amazing, and Paderno, an Italian company, produces another fantastic line. Both are on the pricey side, but if you are a firm believer that you get what you pay for, then their cookware is worth every penny. In a medium price range Le Creuset and All-Clad are outstanding. You can often find sets on sale for a few hundred bucks, or you can assemble your own set as your budget allows. When assessing cookware, no matter what you're buying, there are a few things that you always want to look for. First, that the cookware has an all-metal construction (no plastic handles) so it can go from the stove to the oven to the dishwasher. You'll be amazed by how much time it saves if you can "pan-roast" a chicken breast by sautéing it first then finishing it in the oven.

Second, make sure that your cookware has a thick, heavy bottom for proper heat distribution. Cast-iron skillets have been a kitchen staple for hundreds of years, for good reason: Thin-bottomed pans get hot spots and don't cook evenly (i.e., they burn things). Lastly, it's a good idea to spring for stainless steel—it's simply easier to clean.

A few quality kitchen tools

To put together this list of kitchen tools I simply went to my kitchen and took inventory of the gadgets and tools were I used in creating the recipes for this book.

Flat spatula
Rubber spatula
Slotted fish spatula (Peltex)
Wooden spoons
Slotted spoon
Wire whisk
Fine mesh strainer
Box grater
Measuring spoons
Measuring cups
Wine opener
Pastry brush
Cutting boards
Tongs

Kitchen towels
Kitchen string
Wooden skewers
Mixing bowls
Chopsticks
Peppermill
Two 9-inch cake pans
10½-inch tart pan with
    removable bottom
9 × 5-inch loaf pan
Cookie sheets
Muffin tin
Wok with lid
Roasting pan with rack insert

Grill pan
Pots and skillets
Electric rice cooker
Bamboo steamer
Immersion blender
Tabletop electric mixer
Food processor
Coffee grinder
Whetstone
Oyster knives
Mise en place bowls: small to
    medium bowls to hold
    prepped ingredients

The Pantry

If you don't have at least a modestly stocked pantry, you'll never be able to cook more than an omelet without a trip to the store. With a well-stocked pantry you can cook with confidence and think on your feet at the market. The first thing to do is ask yourself, What kind of food do I like? Italian, Thai, Japanese, Latin American—whatever part of the world your taste buds gravitate toward, that's what you should have on hand.

Asian Pantry

Wasabi powder
White miso
Low-sodium soy sauce
Hoisin sauce
Oyster sauce
Sambal (chili sauce)
Sesame oil
Peanut oil
Rice wine vinegar
Chinese black vinegar
Sake
Plum wine
Mirin (sweet rice wine)
Panko bread crumbs
Cornstarch
Sesame seeds
Short-grain sushi rice
Five-spice powder
Nori (seaweed sheets for sushi)
Bonito flakes (dried tuna)

Thai Pantry

Fish sauce (nam pla)
Coconut milk
Green curry paste
Red curry paste
Lemongrass
Dried chiles
Jasmine rice
Kaffir lime leaves
Soy sauce
Peanuts

Latin Pantry

Extra-virgin olive oil
Sherry vinegar
Canned chipotles in adobo
Dried chiles, such as ancho
Chile powder
Cayenne
Cinnamon
Cumin seed
Sweet paprika
Saffron
Dried oregano
Green olives
Almonds
Rice
Canned black beans
Chocolate

Italian Pantry

Extra-virgin olive oil
Red wine vinegar
Balsamic vinegar
Anchovies
Capers
Raisins
Red pepper flakes
Dried oregano
Bay leaves
Dried pasta: fettuccine, spaghetti, penne
Canned cannellini beans
Canned whole plum tomatoes (San Marzano)
Tomato paste
Arborio rice
Cornmeal for polenta
Assorted olives: black and green
Pine nuts
Walnuts

Herbs and Spices

For me, there is no comparison between fresh herbs and dried—I use only fresh. They add an intense, bright flavor to foods and are widely available. With the exception of oregano, I think dried herbs taste muddy.

Winter herbs, such as rosemary, sage, thyme, and bay leaves, lend themselves to heartier foods (such as Chicken Pot Pie, page 50, or Beef Bourguignon, page 136). These herbs add an earthy depth and hold up to braising or other long slow-cooking processes. In fact, you can't really eat these herbs raw. Cooking releases their natural oils and mellows their intense flavor. Summer herbs, on the other hand, have a sunny flavor punch and are generally better if chopped and tossed in the dish at the last minute. Some of my favorites are basil, cilantro, tarragon, and chives.

Dried spices are a flavor vehicle for taking a dish anywhere you want it to go. Certain spice combinations are indigenous to particular regions. Clove, coriander, and fennel seed say Morocco (see Roasted Chicken with Moroccan Spices, page 53), while cumin, paprika, and cinnamon say Latin America (Arroz con Pollo, page 160). The key to getting optimum flavor from your spices is replacing them regularly— if you have spices that predate the current president, they've got to go. Store spices in airtight containers away from sunlight and oven heat. After sitting on your supermarket shelf losing potency, commercially ground spices may already be past their prime. I prefer buying whole spices and grinding them myself with a coffee grinder that I use only for this purpose. Unless you enjoy freshly ground coffee with a cumin zing, I would definitely have two grinders. This gives you the freedom and ability to create your own spice mixes. Grinding whole spices releases their natural oils on the spot.

★ > ¶O¶   Throughout the book you will see this symbol indicating how long it will take to make a given recipe, start to finish, grocery bag to plate. Don't be intimidated if you pick a recipe that says it takes 2 hours or more. Good food takes time, but not all of that will be hands-on chopping, stirring, sautéing time; some will be standing back, letting things simmer, bake, or chill time. And these estimates are generous; even if you're a fairly new cook you should be able to complete these recipes comfortably within the time indicated, and I promise you it will be time well spent.

"Cooking is truly the one thing that makes the world go round. Behind every culture, there is a real kitchen."

table_
for_
two_

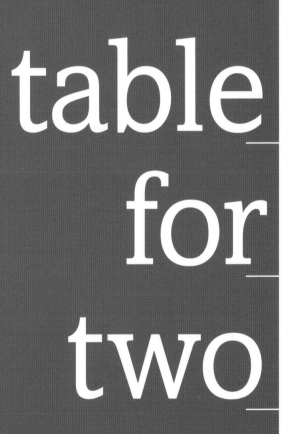

I know how tough it is to cook something after a long day at work, but the alternatives—expensive dinners out, ordering in, frozen whatever, or worse—are not exactly appetizing. So before you order takeout sushi again, consider these quick-to-make classics.

Most are designed to be made in an hour or less using a minimum of pots and pans. And with their simple, clean flavors, you'll emerge from the kitchen looking like a champ every time.

Pan-Fried Tofu with Spinach, Pear, and Star Anise

 **1 hour**

This visually stunning dish also packs a real flavor punch. Even people who don't normally like tofu feast on this dish, though you can substitute beef, if you must. If you can get your hands on an Asian pear, use it here. Green beans are also good in this instead of the spinach. Serve this with Perfect Steamed Jasmine Rice (page 240).

Serves 2

1 block extra-firm tofu, 15 ounces, halved horizontally
2 tablespoons peanut oil
1 tablespoon sesame oil
1½ teaspoons minced fresh ginger, peeled
1 garlic clove, minced
1 fresh red chile, cut in paper-thin circles

3 whole star anise
⅓ cup roasted peanuts
2 tablespoons hoisin sauce
1 tablespoon low-sodium soy sauce
Juice of ½ lime
2 pounds baby spinach
1 pear or Asian pear, sliced into thin wedges

Lay several layers of paper towels on a cutting board, then place the tofu squares on top, side by side. Cover the tofu with more paper towels and place a plate on top. Add a can or two to press down and drain out some of the water in the curd. This makes the tofu denser and meatier.

In a large skillet, heat the peanut and sesame oils just to the smoking point. Fry the tofu on both sides, flipping occasionally with the spatula, until golden, about 8 minutes total. Remove the tofu from the pan and drain it on a plate lined with paper towels.

Using the same pan, sauté the ginger, garlic, chile, star anise, and peanuts—your kitchen will smell amazing! In a small bowl, mix the hoisin sauce, soy sauce, and lime juice together. Briefly toss the spinach in the pan, stirring just to wilt, no more than 30 seconds. Remove the spinach to a bowl, scraping the peanut mixture in there also. Put the pan back on the heat and heat the hoisin mixture. Combine the sauce with the spinach and divide between 2 bowls. Lay the pear slices and tofu on top.

Spaghetti with Peas and Pancetta

 **1 hour**   Photo on page 18

The flavor of peas and bacon takes me back to my childhood; that's why I like this pasta dish so much. I feel like a little kid wolfing this down. It's even good cold!

Serves 2

½ pound spaghetti

Extra-virgin olive oil

6 ounces pancetta or thick-cut bacon, diced

1 onion, minced

1 bay leaf

1 cup sweet peas, frozen or fresh (see Note, page 52)

1 ounce goat cheese

½ cup freshly grated Parmigiano-Reggiano

¼ cup chopped fresh flat-leaf parsley

Juice of 1 lemon

Freshly ground black pepper

¼ cup fresh basil, hand-torn

In a large stockpot, cook the spaghetti in plenty of boiling salted water for about 10 minutes; it should still be a little firm.

At the same time, heat a 2-count drizzle of olive oil in a large skillet over medium-low heat. Add the pancetta, and stir it around. When the fat starts to render, after about 3 minutes, add the onion and bay leaf. Cook and stir until the onion caramelizes, about 10 minutes. Now add the peas and cook for 2 minutes just to heat them through.

Drain the pasta, reserving 1 cup of the starchy water for the sauce. Fold the goat cheese into the hot pasta and give it a toss so it melts. Scrape the pancetta, onions, and peas into the pasta pot (toss the bay leaf). Add the Parmigiano, parsley, and lemon juice. Slowly pour in the reserved pasta water to dissolve the cheese and thin it out to a sauce consistency. Hit it with a healthy dose of olive oil and quite a few turns of freshly ground black pepper to give it bite. Return the noodles to the pot and gently toss to coat in the sauce. Split the pasta between 2 large bowls and shower it with the shredded basil.

Sage-Roasted Pork Tenderloin with Dried Plum Sauce

 **1 hour**

Pork tenderloin is like the filet mignon of the pig, so I serve this with Red Onions Roasted with Balsamic and Honey (page 260) and round everything out with Garlic-Chive Mashed Potatoes (page 237). Charred red onions match perfectly with the sweetness of the dried plums (dried plum is code for prune).

Serves 2

Plum Sauce

1 bottle fruity red wine, such as Pinot Noir
⅓ cup sugar
2 tablespoons red wine vinegar
¾ cup pitted prunes
Sea salt and freshly ground black pepper

Pork Tenderloin

4 fresh sage leaves
1 pound pork tenderloin
Sea salt and freshly ground black pepper
Extra-virgin olive oil

Start with the plum sauce, because it takes longer than the pork. Combine the red wine, sugar, vinegar, and prunes in a pot. Cook over medium heat until the prunes simmer down and get really soft, about 20 minutes. While that is cooking, move on to the pork.

Preheat the oven to 400°F. Arrange the sage sprigs in a row down the length of the pork tenderloin and tie with butcher's twine to hold them in place. Season the pork all over with salt and pepper. Put a cast-iron (or regular ovenproof) skillet over medium-high heat. Coat the bottom of the pan with a little olive oil and get it almost smoking. Add the pork to the pan and sear on all sides until nicely browned and caramelized. Transfer the whole thing to the oven, pan and all, and roast the pork for 10 to 12 minutes.

Puree the prune mixture in a food processor or with a handheld blender. The prunes will thicken the sauce; season with salt and pepper. Cut the string off the pork but leave the sage leaves in place. Slice the pork tenderloin on a slight bias into 1-inch-thick pieces. Drizzle the sauce over the pork.

Pan-Roasted Sirloin with Salad of Arugula, Sweet Peppers, and Olives

 **1 hour**

Avoid using a salad spinner to wash and dry the arugula—the leaves bruise easily. Instead, dunk them in a sink of cool water and lift them into a colander. Pat dry with a kitchen towel. Simple salt and pepper will form a crust on the steaks when you sear them. I don't normally serve anything else with this warm steak salad except the rest of the bottle of Cabernet used in the vinaigrette recipe.

Serves 2

Salad

2 red bell peppers
Extra-virgin olive oil
Sea salt and freshly ground black pepper
1 cup mixed whole black and green olives, such as kalamata and Picholine
1 bunch baby arugula, trimmed
Juice of ½ lemon
4 ounces blue cheese, crumbled

Steak

2 New York strip steaks, 8 to 10 ounces each, about 1½ inches thick
Sea salt and freshly ground black pepper
Extra-virgin olive oil
4 fresh thyme sprigs
½ cup dry red wine, such as Cabernet Sauvignon
½ teaspoon sugar

Start by preparing the peppers because they will take the longest. Preheat the broiler. Pull out their cores, then halve the peppers lengthwise, and remove the ribs and seeds. Toss the peppers with a little olive oil, salt, and pepper. Place them on a cookie sheet, skin side up, and broil for 10 minutes until really charred and blistered. Put the peppers into a bowl, cover with plastic wrap, and let steam for about 10 minutes to loosen the skins. In the meantime, move on to the steaks.

Switch the oven from broil to bake and set the temperature to 350°F. Season both sides of the steaks with sea salt and a generous amount of coarsely ground black pepper, about 1 tablespoon of pepper per steak. Place a cast-iron (or regular ovenproof) skillet over medium-high heat. Coat the bottom of the pan with a 2-count drizzle of olive oil and get it smoking hot. Add the steaks and sear for 4 minutes on each side. Throw in the thyme, then transfer the skillet to the hot oven and roast the steaks for 5 minutes for a nice medium-rare (120 to 125°F. internal temperature).

While that's going, pull the loosened skins off the peppers; cut the peppers into nice fat strips and toss them with the olives. Set aside because the steaks should be ready now. Remove the steaks to a cutting board and let them rest for a few minutes before slicing. (This keeps the juices in the meat, not running all over the counter.)

The last thing to make is a quick vinaigrette using the flavors left in the bottom of the skillet. Pour out some of the beef fat and return the pan to the stove. Add the red wine and boil over medium heat while scraping with a wooden spoon to pull the flavors up. Let the wine reduce to ¼ cup; this will intensify the flavor. Add the sugar and a 1-count of olive oil to balance it out.

Putting it all together is a snap. Cut the steaks on an angle into slices. Gently toss the peppers and olives with the arugula. Drizzle the salad with a little more olive oil, a squeeze of lemon juice, salt, and pepper. Toss lightly again and then divide between 2 plates. Arrange the steak slices on top of the salad and garnish with the crumbled blue cheese; then drizzle the pan vinaigrette over the steak salads and serve.

Creamed Chicken with Mushrooms, Spring Onions, and Leggy Red Wine

 **1½ hours**

I love this dish for the simple ingredients and hearty, rustic flavors. Braising the chicken in red wine actually tenderizes the meat, as well as imparting a beautiful purple hue. "Leggy" red wine means to me a heavy wine with depth and body. Depending on whether or not each of you can eat half a chicken, you will probably have leftovers. Soft, creamy polenta (page 244) is a great accompaniment.

Serves 2

1 chicken, about 3 pounds, cut into 8 pieces

Sea salt and freshly ground black pepper

1½ cups all-purpose flour

Extra-virgin olive oil

2 fresh rosemary sprigs

1 pint white mushrooms, stemmed

3 garlic cloves, minced

1 bottle full-bodied red wine, such as Cabernet Sauvignon

1 tablespoon sugar

½ cup heavy cream

6 spring onions, white and green parts, trimmed

Season the chicken with a fair amount of salt and pepper. Dredge the chicken in the flour and tap off the excess. Place a heavy Dutch oven over medium heat. Coat the bottom with a 2-count of oil. Brown the chicken, skin side down, to crisp the skin. Throw a sprig of rosemary in to create a base flavor. Then turn the chicken over and brown the other side. If the pan looks crowded, do this in batches.

Remove the chicken to a side plate. Add the mushrooms and garlic to the chicken drippings left in the pot; stir until they begin to soften. Pour in the wine and let it cook down, uncovered, until reduced by half. Taste and add the sugar to balance out the tannins in the wine. Return the chicken to the pan, cover, and simmer for about 25 minutes. Remove from heat, stir in the cream, and taste for salt and pepper. The sauce should be thick enough to coat the back of a spoon; if not, cook a few minutes longer. Toss the green onions in for the last few minutes so they are wilted but don't lose their color. Big flavor!

Herb-and-Lemon–Roasted Chicken with Smashed Broccoli and Garlic

 1¼ hours to make + 5 hours to marinate

Give yourself plenty of time to marinate the chicken; I usually do this the morning I plan to serve it. The smashed broccoli and garlic remind me of the soft, overcooked vegetables of my youth. It's mushy and satisfying. To me, chicken and broccoli is a classic combination that doesn't need rice or potatoes to go with—it's perfect the way it is.

Serves 2

Chicken

1 cup extra-virgin olive oil

Zest of 1 lemon, peeled in big strips

4 garlic cloves, smashed

4 fresh thyme sprigs

2 fresh rosemary sprigs

2 bay leaves

2 tablespoons finely chopped fresh chives

2 tablespoons finely chopped fresh flat-leaf parsley

2 tablespoons finely chopped fresh tarragon

1 lemon, sliced in paper-thin circles

2 bone-in chicken breasts, 8 ounces each, skin on

Sea salt and freshly ground black pepper

½ cup Chicken Stock (page 156)

Juice of ½ lemon

1 tablespoon unsalted butter

Broccoli

2 tablespoons extra-virgin olive oil

Pinch of red pepper flakes

5 garlic cloves, coarsely chopped

1 bunch broccoli, about 1 pound, including stems, coarsely chopped

1 cup Chicken Stock (page 156)

¼ cup plain yogurt

Sea salt and freshly ground black pepper

>>

Start by marinating the chicken because it will take the longest. To infuse the oil with flavor and create a base for the marinade, combine the olive oil with the lemon zest, garlic, thyme, rosemary, and bay leaves in a small pot and place over very low heat. You don't want to fry the herbs, just steep them like you're making tea. When the oil begins to simmer, shut off the heat and let it stand for 10 minutes. Pour the fragrant oil, solid pieces and all, into a bowl and put it in the refrigerator to cool.

Combine the chopped chives, parsley, and tarragon in a small bowl. Stuff 2 lemon slices under the skin of each chicken breast, along with half of the mixed chopped herbs. Put the chicken in a resealable food storage bag and pour in the cool herb oil, turning to coat really well. Toss in the remaining half of the chopped herbs, seal the bag, and refrigerate at least 5 hours or as long as all day.

Remove the chicken from the refrigerator about 15 minutes before cooking so it won't be too cold when it goes into the pan; cold chicken takes longer to cook. Preheat the oven to 350°F. Put a cast-iron (or regular ovenproof) skillet over medium heat. Drizzle the bottom of the pan with a 2-count of olive oil and heat until almost smoking; this will keep the chicken from sticking. Season the chicken with a fair amount of salt and pepper and put it in the pan, skin side down. Cook for 5 minutes or until the skin begins to set and crisp. Flip the chicken and brown another 5 minutes. Flip it yet again, so the skin side is down, and transfer the entire pan to the oven. You want the chicken to render its fat and the skin to crisp up. Roast the chicken for 20 to 25 minutes or until cooked through. While that's in the oven, move on to the broccoli.

Heat the olive oil in a medium pot; add the red pepper flakes and garlic. Throw in the broccoli and toss to coat in the garlic and oil. Pour in the chicken stock, cover, and let the broccoli steam for 10 minutes. When it is quite soft, pulse the broccoli a few times in a food processor, or better yet, use a handheld blender if you have one. The broccoli should be partly smooth and partly chunky. Stir in the yogurt to give the broccoli some body and season with salt and pepper.

Transfer the chicken to a platter and keep it warm while preparing the pan sauce. Pour out all but 1 tablespoon of the rendered chicken fat and return the skillet to the stovetop. Add the chicken stock and lemon juice and cook over medium heat, scraping up the flavors with a wooden spoon. Cook the liquid down to a syrup, about 5 minutes. Stir in the butter to smooth out the sauce and turn off the heat.

Spoon the smashed broccoli onto 2 plates, lay the chicken on top, and drizzle with the pan sauce. This is comfort food!

Hong Kong Crab Cakes with Baby Bok Choy

 **1½ hours**

Hong Kong is a truly eye-popping place for a food lover. The dai pai dong *(food stalls) around Stanley Street on Hong Kong Island are full of noodle shops, fishmongers, live chickens, and a dazzling display of the strangest produce I have ever seen. The whole place smells like ginger and fresh coriander—I had a blast. When I got back to New York I was playing around with some of the flavors that I had experienced and came up with these crab cakes. Although crab cakes are not exactly Chinese, the flavors are pure Hong Kong. These crab cakes can easily be prepared ahead of time. Serve with Perfect Steamed Jasmine Rice (page 240).*

Makes 4 crab cakes ★ Serves 2

Crab Cakes

2 garlic cloves, minced

1 tablespoon grated fresh ginger

Peanut oil

1 pound lump crabmeat, preferably Dungeness, picked over for shells

1 cup fresh bread crumbs (see Note)

1 green onion, finely chopped, white and green parts

2 tablespoons mayonnaise

1½ teaspoons red chili paste, such as sambal

Juice of 1 lemon

1 egg white

Sea salt and ground white pepper

Bok Choy

Peanut oil

2-inch piece fresh ginger

2 heads baby bok choy, halved lengthwise

¼ cup low-sodium soy sauce

¼ cup oyster sauce

Juice of ½ lemon

2 tablespoons brown sugar

Toasted sesame seeds (see Note), chopped cilantro, and sliced green onion, for garnish

Sauté the garlic and ginger in a tablespoon of peanut oil for a few minutes; cooking them first really releases a lot of flavor and gives the crab cakes depth. Remove from the heat. In a mixing bowl, combine the crabmeat, bread crumbs, green onion, mayonnaise, chili paste, lemon juice, and egg white. Scrape the garlic-ginger oil into the bowl; season with salt and pepper. Fold the ingredients together gently but thoroughly, taking care not to mash the crabmeat. Using your hands, form the mixture into 4 crab cakes; they should be moist and just hold together. Put the crab cakes on a plate, cover with plastic wrap, and refrigerate while preparing the bok choy. This allows the flavors to blend and the crab cakes to set.

Cover the bottom of a skillet with a 2-count drizzle of peanut oil and heat until almost smoking. Split the piece of ginger open with a knife, then whack it with the flat side of the knife to release the flavor. Lay the ginger pieces in the oil, cut-side down, to let them start to perfume. Pan-fry the bok choy, cut-side down, for a couple of minutes to give it some color. Add the soy sauce, oyster sauce, lemon juice, and brown sugar. Thin out the sauce with ¼ cup of water. Cook for 5 minutes, or until the sauce has a syrupy consistency.

While that's happening, coat another skillet with a 4-count of peanut oil and bring it to a slight smoke over medium heat. Fry the crab cakes until brown, about 5 minutes on each side, turning carefully with a spatula. Serve the crab cakes with the bok choy and garnish with the toasted sesame seeds, cilantro, and green onion.

Notes: *To make fresh bread crumbs: Cut the crusts off some stale bread and pulse it in a food processor.*

To toast sesame seeds: Put the sesame seeds in a dry skillet. Place over medium-low heat and shake the pan constantly until the seeds are golden brown.

I shop only at stores that have the freshest food. When the recipe is simple and the ingredients are impeccable, you don't have to do much to them. Just let the natural flavors speak for themselves."

Slow-Baked Salmon with Asparagus and Honey-Onion Marmalade

 **1 hour**

I am a big fan of flavor on a plate that's light and effortless. I don't need a "balanced" dinner with starch and the whole bit; just give me stuff that tastes good. The delicate flavors of the herbs go great with the salmon and asparagus. It's hard to believe a dish that takes only an hour has such big flavor. Cooking the salmon by the "low and slow" method keeps this fatty fish really moist.

Serves 2

Salmon and Asparagus

¼ bunch fresh flat-leaf parsley

¼ bunch fresh chives

¼ bunch fresh tarragon

¼ bunch fresh cilantro

1½ teaspoons dry mustard

Juice of 1 lemon

¼ cup plus 3 tablespoons canola oil

Sea salt and freshly ground black pepper

2 salmon fillets, 6 to 8 ounces each, skin removed, about 1 inch thick

1 bunch asparagus, stems trimmed

Marmalade

1 tablespoon canola oil

1 Vidalia onion, sliced

2 tablespoons orange juice

1½ teaspoons honey

Sea salt and freshly ground black pepper

Preheat the oven to 250°F. and line a baking pan with aluminum foil. Combine the herbs, dry mustard, lemon juice, and ¼ cup of the canola oil in a blender or food processor and pulse to make a puree. Season the puree with salt and pepper and set aside to let the flavors marry. Place both the fish and asparagus in a baking pan and drizzle them with the remaining 3 tablespoons of canola oil; season with salt and pepper. Bake the salmon and asparagus for 20 minutes. While they cook, make the marmalade.

Heat a skillet over medium-low heat. Coat the pan with oil and add the onion. Add a couple of table-spoons of water to help the onion break down and slowly cook it, stirring, until it caramelizes and releases natural sugars, about 20 minutes. When very soft and cooked down, stir in the orange juice and honey. Season with salt and pepper. The mixture should have the consistency of marmalade.

Remove the salmon and asparagus from the oven. Drizzle the salmon and asparagus with the herb puree and serve with the honey-onion marmalade on the side. Garnish the plate with a few fresh herbs.

Braised Red Snapper with Grandma-Style Zucchini, Peppers, and Black Olives

 **under 1 hour**

"Grandma-style" means the vegetables are cooked like a stew in a big pot until they're soft and deli-cious. The vegetables taste better and better as you cook them down, and the broth tastes nourishing. This is one of the classic recipes I pull out in a pinch, and it's always welcomed.

Serves 2

3 red bell peppers

Extra-virgin olive oil

Sea salt and freshly ground black pepper

15 baby new potatoes, halved

3 zucchini, cut in ½-inch-thick circles

½ cup whole kalamata olives

3 garlic cloves, sliced

2 fresh thyme sprigs

6 fresh tarragon leaves

½ lemon, sliced paper-thin

2 cups Chicken Stock (page 156)

1 cup dry white wine, such as Sauvignon Blanc

Juice of 1 lemon

2 center-cut red snapper fillets, about 8 ounces each, skin on, halved on the diagonal

Preheat the broiler. Pull out the cores of the red peppers; then halve them lengthwise and remove the ribs and seeds. Toss the peppers with a little olive oil, salt, and pepper. Place them on a cookie sheet, skin side up, and broil for 10 minutes, until really charred and blistered. Put the peppers into a bowl, cover with plastic wrap, and steam for about 10 minutes to loosen the skins. Peel the peppers and cut them into big strips.

Heat a 2-count of oil in a wide pot. Add the roasted peppers, potatoes, zucchini, olives, garlic, thyme, tarragon, and lemon slices. Sauté everything together for a few minutes over medium heat to coat in the oil and soften; season with salt and pepper. Add the chicken stock, wine, and lemon juice. Bring to a boil, then reduce the heat, and let it slowly simmer down for 30 minutes while you prepare the fish.

Rub a little olive oil and salt and pepper on the fish fillets. Add a 2-count drizzle of olive oil to a skillet and place over medium heat. When the pan is nice and hot, sear the fish, skin side down. Gently press on the fish with a spatula to crisp up the skin. Carefully transfer the fish to the pot of vegetables, skin side up. Turn the heat down to low, cover, and simmer for 5 minutes. Keep an eye on it; don't let the liquid boil or cook the fish too long or it will fall apart. Serve the fish and vegetables in wide, shallow bowls with a ladle of broth and a drizzle of olive oil. Home-style goodness!

Seared Tuna with Chinese Salad and Ginger-Soy Vinaigrette

 **1 hour**

Salads are quick and painless to throw together on a work night, and you won't feel like you'll have to do double time at the gym the next day. If you're on your own, this is also a speedy and healthy dinner for one: Just use one tuna steak and a few less vegetables. The colors of this sophisticated and simple salad really pop. I like hothouse cucumbers because they have minimal seeds and tender skin. The mustard packets that you get from Chinese takeout are really put to good use in this Asian vinaigrette.

Serves 2

Vinaigrette

3 tablespoons low-sodium soy sauce

Juice of 1 lime

Splash of rice wine vinegar

2 teaspoons grated fresh ginger

4 teaspoons Chinese mustard

1 tablespoon honey

⅓ cup canola oil

1 tablespoon sesame oil

Freshly ground black pepper

Salad

½ head Chinese cabbage, such as napa or Savoy, shredded

1 bunch watercress, hand-torn

¼ cup chopped fresh cilantro

1 hothouse cucumber, sliced thin

2 green onions, sliced on the diagonal, white and green parts

2 radishes, sliced in circles

1 carrot, sliced thin

¼ cup radish sprouts (optional)

¼ cup slivered almonds, toasted

½ cup canned mandarin orange segments, drained

Tuna

2 sushi-quality tuna steaks, such as ahi (yellowfin), 6 to 8 ounces each

2 tablespoons sesame oil

Sea salt and ground white pepper

½ cup sesame seeds

1 tablespoon canola oil

To make the vinaigrette, whisk together the soy sauce, lime juice, vinegar, ginger, mustard, and honey. Gradually drizzle in both oils, as you constantly whisk, until the dressing thickens and comes together. Add a few twists of freshly ground black pepper to give the vinaigrette bite.

Combine the cabbage, watercress, cilantro, cucumber, green onions, radishes, and carrot in a bowl. Use your hands to toss the salad. Then add the radish sprouts, almonds, and mandarin oranges; lightly toss again. Don't dress the salad yet because it will get soggy. Cover it and put it in the refrigerator while you deal with the tuna; the contrast of chilled salad and warm tuna is fantastic.

Rub both sides of the tuna steaks with 1 tablespoon of the sesame oil, salt, and white pepper. Spread the sesame seeds out on a plate and lightly press each side of the tuna steaks into the seeds. Heat the canola oil and remaining tablespoon of sesame oil in a large skillet over high heat. Lay the steaks in the hot pan. Sear the tuna for about 3 minutes, until the sesame seeds form a crust. Flip the tuna steaks over and cook the other side 3 to 4 minutes longer for rare. Slice the tuna on a slight angle into 1-inch-thick slices.

Toss the salad with half the vinaigrette; season with salt and pepper. Divide the salad between two plates, lay the tuna slices on top, and then drizzle with the remaining dressing. Elegant presentation!

dinner with friends

On the weekends, I love to host dinner parties in my apartment, with big platters of food served family-style, great bottles of wine, good friends, and plenty of laughs. Dinner parties are such a good way to connect with the people in your life and so much more personal than going out to a restaurant.

At my place everybody gets their hands into what's going on in the kitchen. When I'm cooking dinner for six to eight people, I try to keep it simple, and by that I mean making just one thing. Whether it's a big pot of curry or just a great lasagna and a simple salad, the idea is to serve an unpretentious meal with huge flavor. Most of these recipes feed six or eight, they're unfussy to make, and they're really good. So instead of making reservations, make my Thick Pork Chops with Spiced Apples and Raisins and invite some people over.

Chicken Pot Pie

 **2 hours**

Pot pie has come long way. I recently went to a charity event in New York City, at which David Bowie was the guest of honor. The main course? Chicken pot pie. Go figure! Frozen puff pastry sheets work really well here without compromising the dish, but allow an hour or more to thaw the frozen sheets. Serving individual pot pies makes for a great presentation. You can pick the crocks up at any kitchen store or use 2-cup ramekins if you already have them.

Serves 4

Chicken Broth

1 whole chicken, 3 pounds

3 carrots, cut in 2-inch pieces

3 celery stalks, cut in 2-inch pieces

1 onion, halved

1 head garlic, halved horizontally

2 turnips, halved

Bouquet garni: 4 fresh thyme sprigs, 2 fresh
  rosemary sprigs, 1 bay leaf—all tied
  together with kitchen string

Pot Pie

¼ pound (1 stick) unsalted butter

½ cup all-purpose flour

Sea salt and freshly ground black pepper

4 carrots, cut in ½-inch circles

1 cup pearl onions, peeled (see Notes)

1 cup sweet peas, frozen or fresh (see Notes)

Leaves from 4 fresh thyme sprigs

2 frozen puff pastry sheets, thawed

1 egg

¼ cup shredded Parmigiano-Reggiano cheese

Put the chicken in a large stockpot and cover with 1 gallon of cool water. Add the vegetables and herbs and bring the pot up to a boil over medium-high heat. Skim well; then simmer, uncovered, for 45 minutes, skimming frequently as the oil rises to the surface. What we're doing here is not only cooking the chicken but also creating the base sauce for the pot pie. It's the old trick of killing two birds with one stone—or one pot, as the case may be. Remove the chicken to a platter to cool. Continue to cook down the chicken broth for another 15 minutes to condense the flavor; you should have about 8 cups when you're finished. Using a colander, strain the chicken broth into another pot and discard the solids. When the chicken is cool enough to handle, shred the meat and discard the skin and bones.

>>

Wipe out the stockpot and put it back on the stovetop over medium heat. Melt the butter and then whisk in the flour to form a paste. This is a roux, which will act as a thickener. Now, gradually pour in 8 cups of the chicken broth, whisking the entire time to prevent lumps. Whisk and simmer for 10 minutes to cook out the starchy taste of the flour and thicken the broth; it should look like cream of chicken soup. Season with salt and pepper. Fold in the shredded chicken, carrots, pearl onions, peas, and thyme. Stir to combine and turn off the heat.

Preheat the oven to 350°F. Lay the thawed puff pastry sheets on a lightly floured, cool surface. Invert a crock on the pastry sheet and, using a sharp knife, cut circles around the outside of the bowl, slightly larger than the bowl itself. Fill the crocks three-quarters of the way full with the chicken mixture, making sure each serving has a nice amount of chicken, vegetables, and broth. Carefully cap each crock with a pastry circle, pressing the dough around the rim to form a seal. Lightly beat the egg with 3 tablespoons of water to make an egg wash and brush some on the pastry. Sprinkle the pastry with the Parmigiano cheese. Set the crocks on a cookie sheet and transfer to the oven. Bake for 20 minutes, until puffed and golden. Chicken pot pie is such a complete meal that I wouldn't serve it with anything but a nice glass of sauvignon blanc or a cold beer.

Notes: If using fresh pearl onions, blanch for 2 minutes in salted boiling water; then pinch the skins off—if using frozen, run under cool water for 2 minutes to thaw.

If using fresh peas, blanch for 2 minutes in salted boiling water—if using frozen, run under cool water for 2 minutes to thaw.

Roasted Chicken with Moroccan Spices

 **1½ hours**

This is a quick throw-together with intense Moroccan flavor. Cooking the chicken on a rack allows the oven's heat to circulate around the bird and cook it faster. Serve the chicken with Baked Eggplant with Sesame Yogurt and Mint (page 262).

Serves 4

1 whole chicken, 3½ pounds

1 cinnamon stick, chopped in pieces

8 whole cloves

1 teaspoon cayenne

2 teaspoons cumin seed

1 teaspoon fennel seed

1 teaspoon coriander seed

1 tablespoon sweet paprika

1½ teaspoons sea salt

1 teaspoon brown sugar

Sea salt and freshly ground black pepper

1 lemon, halved

¼ bunch fresh cilantro

2 garlic cloves

3 tablespoons extra-virgin olive oil

Preheat the oven to 400°F. Rinse the chicken with cool water inside and out; then pat it dry with paper towels. Combine the cinnamon stick, cloves, cayenne, cumin, fennel, coriander, and paprika in a dry skillet over low heat and toast for just a minute to release the fragrant oils; shake the pan so the spices don't scorch. In a spice mill or clean coffee grinder, grind the toasted spices together with the sea salt and brown sugar.

Massage the chicken skin with the spice rub; make sure you don't miss a spot. Season the inside of the chicken generously with salt and pepper. Stuff the lemons halves, cilantro, and garlic in the cavity. Place the chicken in a roasting pan fitted with a rack. Fold the wing tips under the bird and tie the legs together with kitchen string. Drizzle the oil all over the chicken. If you have time, let the chicken sit for 30 minutes to really get the flavors deep into the meat. Roast the chicken for 1 hour, then pop an instant-read thermometer into the thickest part of the thigh; if it reads 160°F, it's time to eat. Allow the chicken to rest for 10 minutes before carving so the juices can settle back into the meat. Squeeze the lemon halves that have cooked inside the chicken over the meat for added pow.

Wok-Smoked Duck with Green Tea and Orange

 1½ hours + 24 hours marinating time

This dish takes a little planning ahead but is well worth it. Don't be scared—it's a show-off dish. You may, however, have to shop around for some of the makings. A trip to your local Asian market or a surf on the Internet should do it. Start by marinating the duck the night before you plan to serve it. A smoker isn't required, but you will need a wok with a domed lid and wire rack insert (sorry, an electric wok won't work). Serve with steamed Asian greens like bok choy or Chinese broccoli. Round out the meal with Perfect Steamed Jasmine Rice (page 240).

Serves 4

Duck

1 whole duck, 5 pounds
2 cups low-sodium soy sauce
1 cup water
1 cup honey
3-inch piece fresh ginger, coarsely chopped
4 garlic cloves, smashed
⅓ cup brown sugar
1 orange, halved
1 lemon, halved
1 lime, halved

Smoker

1 cup raw jasmine rice
½ cup loose green tea
¼ cup sugar

Orange Glaze

2 cups plum wine
¼ cup rice wine vinegar
½ cup water
½ teaspoon cornstarch
1-inch piece fresh ginger, cut into paper-thin slices
Peel and juice of 1 orange
1 tablespoon low-sodium soy sauce
1 garlic clove, halved
Sea salt and ground white pepper

2 tablespoons toasted sesame seeds, for garnish (see Note, page 34)

Pierce the skin of the duck with a fork so the flavor of the marinade can penetrate the meat. In a large bowl, whisk together the soy sauce, water, honey, ginger, garlic, and brown sugar. Squeeze in the juice of the orange, lemon, and lime, reserving the empty rinds. Place the duck in a 2-gallon plastic storage bag, pour in the marinade, and toss in the citrus halves. Seal and refrigerate for 24 hours. The next afternoon, take the duck out of the marinade and pat it dry with paper towels. Stuff the duck cavity with the marinated citrus rinds and discard the rest of the marinade. Fold the wing tips under and tie the legs together with kitchen string. The duck should have a dark coffee color and smell of citrus and ginger.

The next thing you want to work on is setting up the wok-smoker. Line the bottom of the wok with a piece of heavy-duty aluminum foil. Spread the rice, green tea, and sugar on the foil in an even layer and place the wok on the stovetop. Set the steamer rack insert on top of the foil and turn the heat to high. When the rice starts to smoke, lay the duck on the rack, breast side up. Lower the heat to medium-low and cover tightly with the domed lid. The goal is to impart a sweet, smoky flavor to the duck. Let the duck hot smoke for 20 minutes; then turn the heat off and leave the duck covered in the chamber of smoke for another 10 minutes. You will see and smell a fragrant smoke creeping out from under the lid. As tempting as it is, do not peek under the lid, because all the smoke will escape and with it the smoky flavor.

Preheat the oven to 375°F. Take the lid off the wok, set the duck on a plate, remove the rack, and discard the foil with the rice. The wok can now be transformed into a roasting pan. Put the rack back inside the wok, place the duck on top, and put the whole thing in the oven without the lid. Roast the duck for 1 hour to crisp the skin and set its deep mahogany color. The legs will jiggle easily when the duck is done.

As the duck roasts, make the sauce. In a pot over medium-low heat, combine the plum wine, rice wine vinegar, water, cornstarch, ginger, orange peel and juice, soy sauce, and garlic. Cook down for about 15 to 20 minutes, until the sauce thickens enough to coat the back of a spoon. Season with salt and white pepper.

With a very sharp knife or cleaver, carve the duck and arrange the pieces on a serving platter. Spoon the sauce over the duck and garnish with the sesame seeds.

Green Curry Chicken

 **1 hour**

If you have never experimented with Thai ingredients before, try this recipe—the flavors are mental. Lemongrass, coconut milk, basil, lime: They all hit the palate in perfect harmony. If you love Thai food, this is a great dish to start playing around with—and it's very easy. The floral aroma of green curry simmering on the stove is hypnotic. Kaffir lime leaves are crucial to this dish and are worth the trip to your local Asian market. Serve with Perfect Steamed Jasmine Rice (page 240).

Serves 4

Canola oil

1 onion, cut in 8 wedges

2 green bell peppers, cut in 8 wedges

1 stalk lemongrass, white bulb only

1 tablespoon minced fresh ginger

4 teaspoons green curry paste

6 kaffir lime leaves

2½ cups unsweetened coconut milk

¼ cup Chicken Stock (page 156)

Juice of 1 lime

1½ pounds skinless, boneless chicken breasts, cut in 1-inch strips

Sea salt

⅓ cup coarsely chopped basil leaves

⅓ cup coarsely chopped cilantro

Lime wedges, for garnish

Place a large, deep skillet over medium heat and coat with a 2-count drizzle of oil. Sauté the onion and green peppers for 3 minutes to soften. Split the pieces of lemongrass down the middle and whack them with the flat side of a knife to open the flavor. Add the lemongrass, ginger, curry paste, and lime leaves to the skillet and stir for 2 minutes. Add the coconut milk, chicken stock, and lime juice. Lay the chicken pieces in the mixture to poach; add a pinch of salt. Stir the whole thing together and simmer over low heat for 15 minutes. Shower chopped basil, cilantro, and another pinch of salt over the chicken; then serve in dinner bowls with lime wedges. Big flavor!

Thick Pork Chops with Spiced Apples and Raisins

 1½ hours to make + 2 hours to brine

One trick that I learned a long time ago about cooking pork is that you have to brine it. The brine for this recipe is a sugar-salt solution mixed with apple juice concentrate (you will need 2 cans of frozen juice) for the brine and spiced apples. With its sweet apple flavor, this is an intense marinade that works miracles on pork chops. Trust me—once you taste a thick pork chop that's been flavored in a brine, you will never go back. Cozy up to your butcher to get the pork chops cut to your liking. Thin pork chops—no way! Serve this with Corn Pudding (page 236).

Serves 4

Pork Chops

1 gallon water

1 cup brown sugar

1 cup sea salt

1 cup frozen apple juice concentrate, thawed

1½ teaspoons whole black peppercorns

2 fresh thyme sprigs

4 double-cut bone-in loin pork chops, 1 pound each

Sea salt and freshly ground black pepper

Extra-virgin olive oil

Spiced Apples and Raisins

2 tablespoons unsalted butter

3 Granny Smith apples, peeled, cored, and sliced in ½-inch-thick wedges

Leaves from 2 fresh thyme sprigs

¼ cup raisins

¾ cup frozen apple juice concentrate, thawed

3 tablespoons brown sugar

¼ teaspoon ground cinnamon

¼ teaspoon ground cloves

Pinch of cardamom

Pinch of dry mustard

Sea salt and freshly ground black pepper

Juice of ½ lemon

Combine the water, brown sugar, sea salt, apple juice, peppercorns, and thyme in an extra-large plastic bag. Give it a stir to dissolve the sugar and salt. Submerge the pork chops in the brine, seal up the bag, and put it in the refrigerator for 2 hours to tenderize the meat. Do not brine longer than that or the meat will break down too much and get mushy.

Preheat the oven to 350°F. Remove the pork chops from the brine and pat them dry with paper towels. Sprinkle both sides of the meat with salt and pepper. Put a heavy skillet over medium-high heat. Add a 3-count drizzle of olive oil and get it hot. Lay 2 pork chops in the pan (most likely only 2 of these massive pork chops will fit comfortably) and brown 4 minutes per side. Remove the pork chops to a large baking pan; brown the remaining 2 chops and add them to the others in the pan. Put the baking pan in the oven and roast the chops for 30 minutes. The pork is done when the center is still rosy and the internal temperature reads 140° to 145°F. when tested with an instant-read thermometer.

While the chops cook, melt the butter in a clean skillet over medium-low heat. Add the apples and thyme and coat in the butter; cook and stir for 8 minutes to give them some color. Toss in the raisins and add the apple juice, stirring to scrape up the brown bits. Stir in the brown sugar, cinnamon, cloves, cardamom, and dry mustard; season with salt and pepper. Squeeze in the lemon juice to wake up the flavor and simmer for 10 minutes or until the apples break down and soften. Spoon the spiced apples over the pork chops.

Dad's Meatloaf with Tomato Relish

 **2 hours**

There is no denying that meatloaf is the king of comfort food. Everyone loves meatloaf but is afraid to admit it. Trust me, before heading out the door your guests will be asking you for your recipe. This is my dad's recipe, and I've been using it for years. This meatloaf was also one of the biggest hits at Cafeteria Restaurant in New York, where I was the chef. Serve this with Garlic-Chive Mashed Potatoes (page 237).

Serves 6 to 8

Tomato Relish

Extra-virgin olive oil

1 onion, finely diced

2 garlic cloves, minced

2 bay leaves

2 red bell peppers, cored, seeded, and finely diced

2 tomatoes, halved, seeded, and finely diced

¼ cup chopped fresh flat-leaf parsley

1 (12-ounce) bottle ketchup

1 tablespoon Worcestershire sauce

Sea salt and freshly ground black pepper

Meatloaf

2½ pounds ground beef

3 eggs

Leaves from 2 fresh thyme sprigs

Sea salt and freshly ground black pepper

¾ to 1 cup fresh bread crumbs (2 or 3 slices stale white bread, crusts removed, pulsed in the food processor)

3 bacon slices

Coat a skillet with a 2-count of oil and place over medium heat. Sauté the onion, garlic, and bay leaves for a few minutes to create a base flavor. Throw in the red peppers and cook them for a couple of minutes to soften. Now add the tomatoes; adding them at this point lets them hold their shape and prevents them from disintegrating. Stir in the parsley, ketchup, and Worcestershire; season with salt and pepper. Simmer the relish for 5 minutes to pull all the flavors together. Remove it from the heat; you should have about 4 cups of relish.

Preheat the oven to 350°F. This is where you get your hands dirty! In a large mixing bowl, combine the ground beef with 1½ cups of the tomato relish, the eggs, and thyme; season with salt and pepper. Add the bread crumbs in stages, starting with ¾ cup; you may not need all of them. To test, fry a small "hamburger" patty of the meatloaf until cooked; the patty should hold together but still have a soft consistency. Taste the patty for seasoning.

Fill a 9 × 5-inch loaf pan with the meat mixture and tap the pan on the counter so it settles. Flatten the top with a spatula and cover with another ½ cup of the tomato relish. Lay the bacon across the top lengthwise. Place the pan on a cookie sheet; this prevents the liquid from dripping and burning on the bottom of the oven. (I also recommend rotating the meatloaf a few times so the bacon browns evenly.)

Bake the meatloaf for 1 to 1½ hours until the bacon is crisp and the meatloaf pulls away from the sides of the pan. Remove the meatloaf from the oven and let it cool a bit before slicing. Serve with the remaining tomato relish on the side. Unbelievably moist!

Roast Prime Rib of Beef with Horseradish Crust and Wild Mushrooms

 **2½ hours**

This is truly the anti-vegetarian dish. Prime rib is one of those classics you can pull out that will always blow people away. It's a good special occasion dish, so good that the occasion may be nothing at all. When ordering the rib roast from a butcher, be sure to request a "top choice" roast cut from the small loin end, the best being ribs 12 through 10. Have the butcher cut off the chine (backbone) to make carving easier. The rib bones look best if they are shortened and frenched (the butcher will be happy to do this for you as well, unless he's a sourpuss, in which case get a new butcher). The wild mushrooms alone make a great all-purpose side dish.

Serves 6 to 8

Prime Rib

1 3-rib prime rib beef roast, about 6 pounds

5 garlic cloves, smashed

¼ cup grated fresh or prepared horseradish

Needles from 2 fresh rosemary sprigs

Leaves from 4 fresh thyme sprigs

½ cup sea salt

¼ cup freshly ground black pepper

½ cup extra-virgin olive oil

4 carrots, cut in chunks

4 parsnips

4 red onions, halved

2 heads of garlic, halved

Wild Mushrooms

1 tablespoon unsalted butter

Extra-virgin olive oil

2 shallots, minced

2 pounds assorted mushrooms, such as crimini, oyster, shiitake, chanterelle, or white, trimmed and sliced

Leaves from 2 fresh thyme sprigs

Sea salt and freshly ground black pepper

½ cup Cabernet Sauvignon

¼ cup reserved beef broth (drippings from roast) or low-sodium canned broth

¼ cup heavy cream

1 tablespoon minced fresh chives

Preheat the oven to 350°F. Lay the beef in a large roasting pan with the bone side down. (The ribs act as a natural roasting rack.) In a small bowl mash together the garlic, horseradish, rosemary, thyme, salt, pepper, and olive oil to make a paste. Massage the paste generously over the entire roast. Scatter the vegetables around the meat and drizzle them with a 2-count of oil. Put the pan in the oven and roast the beef for about 1½ to 2 hours for medium-rare (or approximately 20 minutes per pound). Check the internal temperature of the roast in several places with an instant-read thermometer; it should register 125°F. for medium-rare. Remove the beef to a carving board and let it rest for 20 minutes. The internal temperature of the meat will continue to rise by about 10 degrees. Remove the vegetables and set aside. Pour the pan juices into a fat separator or small bowl and set aside to allow the fat and beef juices to separate. Pour off and discard the fat. You will use the tasty beef juices for the mushrooms.

Place a clean skillet over medium heat. Add the butter and a 2-count drizzle of oil. When the butter starts to foam, add the shallots and sauté for 2 minutes to soften. Add the mushrooms and thyme; season with salt and pepper. Stir everything together for a few minutes. Add the red wine, stirring to scrape up any stuck bits; then cook and stir to evaporate the alcohol. When the wine is almost all gone, add the reserved beef juices. Let the liquid cook down and then take it off the heat. Stir in the cream and chives, and season with salt and pepper.

"It's often been my experience that many of the cleanest, best flavors are very simple ones."

Drop-Dead Lasagna

 **2½ hours**

This is the old-school lasagna that you find in the Italian restaurants in Brooklyn. Fuggedaboudit! You can assemble the lasagna ahead of time . . . and it's great for leftovers.

Serves 12

1 pound ruffled lasagna noodles
Extra-virgin olive oil
1 onion, diced
3 garlic cloves, minced
1 bay leaf
1½ pounds ground beef
1 pound ground pork
1 tablespoon fennel seeds
½ tablespoon red pepper flakes
1 teaspoon brown sugar
½ tablespoon dried oregano
1 (6-ounce) can tomato paste

Sea salt and freshly ground black pepper
2 pounds ricotta cheese
½ cup freshly grated Parmigiano-Reggiano cheese
¼ cup finely chopped fresh flat-leaf parsley
½ cup finely chopped fresh basil
2 eggs, lightly beaten
2 pounds shredded mozzarella cheese
4 cups Marinara Sauce (page 68) or good-quality jarred pasta sauce
Additional Parmigiano-Reggiano for serving

Fill a large pasta pot with water and place over high heat. Add a generous amount of salt and bring to a boil. Cook the lasagna noodles for only 8 minutes; they should still be somewhat firm, as they will continue to cook when you bake the lasagna. Drain the noodles in a colander and rinse them quickly under cool water to stop the cooking process. Drizzle with some olive oil so the sheets don't stick together, then set aside.

Heat a large skillet over medium heat and drizzle with a 2-count of olive oil. Sauté the onion, garlic, and bay leaf for a couple of minutes, until the onions are translucent and smell sweet. Add the ground beef and pork, stirring to break it up, and cook until the meat is thoroughly browned, about 10 minutes. Drain out the excess fat. Combine the fennel seeds, red pepper flakes, brown sugar, and dried oregano in a spice mill or clean coffee grinder; give it a whirl, and sprinkle on the browned meat. Stir in the tomato paste until well blended; season with salt and pepper. Take the pan off the heat.

In a large bowl, combine the ricotta and Parmigiano cheeses. Fold in the parsley, basil, and eggs, season with salt and pepper, and mix well.

Preheat the oven to 350°F. Take inventory of the components you should now have: slightly cooked lasagna noodles, seasoned meat mixture, ricotta cheese filling, 2 pounds of shredded mozzarella cheese, a pot of sauce, and a 13×9-inch glass or ceramic baking dish. Let the layering begin.

Start by ladling enough sauce into the dish to cover the bottom; in my experience, this prevents the lasagna from sticking. Layer 1—the noodles: Slightly overlap 4 lasagna noodles lengthwise so they completely cover the bottom with no gaps. Here is a little tip I swear by: If you take 2 lasagna noodles and line the short ends of the pan, they will act as brackets or a wall to give the lasagna support when you cut it. Layer 2—the meat: Spread half the meat mixture on the top of the noodles with a spatula. The meat mixture, being the most solid element, will act as a foundation. Layer 3—the cheese: Spread half the ricotta cheese mixture over the meat, smooth out with a spatula, and then sprinkle a third of the shredded mozzarella evenly over the ricotta mixture for that stringy cheese pull that you know and love. Layer 4—the sauce: Top with a full ladle of tomato sauce, about 1 cup; smooth it out with a spatula. Repeat layers 1 through 4. Finish with a final layer of noodles, tomato sauce, and the remaining mozzarella. I like to tap the pan lightly on the counter to force out any air bubbles and compress the layers. Bake for $1\frac{1}{2}$ hours, until golden and bubbling. Allow the lasagna to sit for 20 minutes so it doesn't ooze all over the place when you cut it into squares. Pass tomato sauce and grated Parmigiano around the table.

Marinara Sauce

Growing up, my family had a tradition that whoever got the bay leaf had to do the dishes.

* **From grocery bag to plate: 1 hour**
* **makes 5 cups**

Extra-virgin olive oil
1 onion, diced
2 garlic cloves, minced
2 (28-ounce) cans whole plum tomatoes
5 fresh basil leaves, cut in fine ribbons
2 tablespoons chopped fresh flat-leaf parsley
2 bay leaves
Pinch of red pepper flakes
½ teaspoon sugar
Sea salt and freshly ground black pepper

In a large pot over medium heat, heat a 3-count drizzle of oil until hot. Add the onion and garlic and sauté for 5 minutes, or until the onions begin to appear translucent. Hand-crush the tomatoes and add them, along with their liquid, to the pot. Toss in the herbs, red pepper flakes, and sugar; season with salt and pepper. Lower the heat and simmer for 45 minutes, uncovered. Stir occasionally.

Linguine with Sicilian Clam Sauce

 **45 minutes**

The clams in this dish are steamed with tomatoes, fresh basil, and red pepper flakes. The flavors are simple and delicious. Dinner in under an hour never tasted so good.

Serves 4 to 6

Sea salt

1 pound linguine

Extra-virgin olive oil

4 anchovy fillets, chopped

6 garlic cloves, shaved

1 onion, diced

1 teaspoon red pepper flakes

¼ cup capers, drained

1 cup hand-torn fresh basil

2 (28-ounce) cans whole plum tomatoes, drained

48 littleneck clams, scrubbed

½ cup dry white wine

Juice of 1 lemon

Sea salt and freshly ground black pepper

Freshly grated Parmigiano-Reggiano cheese (optional)

Fill a large pasta pot with water and place over high heat. Add a generous amount of salt and bring to a boil. Add the pasta, stir to separate, and cook for 10 minutes, until al dente. Drain well and toss with a little oil so the pasta doesn't stick together.

Heat a 2-count drizzle of olive oil in a large pot and set over medium heat. Add the anchovies, garlic, onion, red pepper flakes, capers, and ½ cup of basil. Sauté for a minute, until fragrant. Hand-crush the tomatoes to break them up into chunks. Pour them into the pan (be careful—nothing splashes quite like tomatoes) and simmer down the tomatoes until pulpy. This will take about 15 minutes. Nestle the clams in the tomato mixture and toss everything together with a large spoon. Pour in the wine and cover the pot to let the clams steam open, about 10 minutes. Add the linguine; then fold in the remaining basil, lemon juice, and some salt and pepper. Give it a good toss with more olive oil. Serve the pasta family-style on a large platter.

Bacon-Wrapped Shrimp with Chunky Tomatillo Salsa and Tomato Vinaigrette

 **45 minutes**

I love bacon and shrimp. It's a classic combination that works really well in this Southwestern-inspired bistro dish.

Serves 4

Tomatillo Salsa

6 tomatillos, husked, rinsed, and cut in chunks

2 avocados, peeled and cut in chunks

2 jalapeños, cut in circles

½ bunch fresh cilantro, coarsely chopped

½ red onion, diced

Juice of 3 limes

2 tablespoons canola oil

Sea salt and freshly ground black pepper

Tomato Vinaigrette

1 ripe tomato, halved, seeds squeezed out

1 canned chipotle pepper in adobo

1 garlic clove

Zest and juice of 1 lime

1 tablespoon sherry vinegar

1 teaspoon sugar

½ teaspoon sea salt

2 tablespoons canola oil

Shrimp

20 large shrimp (about 2 pounds), peeled and deveined, tails on

10 bacon slices, halved

Extra-virgin olive oil

2 green onions, thinly sliced on the diagonal, for garnish

Chopped fresh cilantro, for garnish

For the tomatillo salsa, toss the tomatillos, avocados, jalapeños, cilantro, and onion together in a large bowl. Add the lime juice and canola oil, and turn to coat; season with salt and black pepper. Turn the mixture over a few times until the avocados are slightly mashed and the salsa is creamy. Cover and refrigerate while you prepare everything else.

Puree the tomato, chipotle, garlic, lime zest, lime juice, sherry vinegar, sugar, and salt in a blender until smooth. Pour in the oil and puree again until emulsified and slightly thickened. Refrigerate.

Wrap each shrimp in a piece of bacon, overlapping the ends so they stick together. Place a large skillet over medium heat, drizzle with a ½-count of oil, and heat just to the smoking point. Lay the shrimp in the pan (do this in batches if it's crowded) and sauté until the bacon is crisp, tossing so the shrimp cook evenly. To serve, spoon a mound of the tomatillo salsa on each plate. Drizzle a pool of the tomato vinaigrette and top with 5 shrimp. Garnish with green onion and cilantro leaves. This shrimp dish also works well on the grill with margaritas and a lot of beer.

Sushi

Sushi is truly one of the world's super foods, and every time I have it, I feel like I've done something good for myself.

It's high in protein and complex carbohydrates; I could eat it on a desert island for the rest of my life and be completely happy. The great thing about making sushi for a casual dinner party is that you're not stuck in front of the stove all night, which frees you up to actually have a good time. On top of that, sushi is a snap to make. The recipes in this "subchapter" are simple to make and innovative in presentation, and you will end up looking like a Japanese sushi master. The fish has to be impeccably fresh, so stroll over to the fish market to pick up the very best; and you'll probably need to take a trip to an Asian market, too. Don't forget the Japanese plates and chopsticks, pickled ginger, soy sauce, edamame, sake, and beer.

Spicy Tuna Hand Roll

 30 minutes

Photo on page 78–79

The Japanese man I buy my fish from gave me this recipe. One day I noticed that he was making hand rolls for lunch from the trimmings of a No. 1 grade A tuna loin. He let me have a roll since I'm such a good customer, and I have to say it was the best spicy tuna roll I'd ever had. You'll get the hang of rolling these in no time—practice makes perfect.

Makes 8 pieces

¾ cup mayonnaise

3 tablespoons red chili paste, such as sambal

Juice of ½ lemon

2 tablespoons dried bonito flakes

1 tablespoon flying fish roe (tobiko)

Sea salt

1 pound sushi-quality tuna, such as ahi (yellowfin) or bluefin, cut into ¼-inch cubes

4 sheets nori seaweed

2 cups prepared sushi rice (page 80)

Finely chopped green onion, for garnish

In a small bowl, combine the mayonnaise, chili paste, lemon juice, bonito flakes, fish roe, and a pinch of sea salt. Put the tuna cubes in a mixing bowl and gradually fold in the mayonnaise mixture a little at a time to coat the fish. There will be some left over. Cut the nori sheets in half. Place half a sheet, shiny side down, in the palm of your hand. Dampen your fingers and spread a thin, even layer of sushi rice over half the sheet covering your palm side. Spoon a generous tablespoon of the spicy tuna down the center of the rice. Now, read this next part a few times before you attempt it—it's a little tricky: To form a cone, start with the inner corner that is closest to the palm of your hand. Fold it in toward the center of the paper, covering the rice. Continue to roll until it forms a cone; then dab the far edge with a little water to seal the cone. Top it off with a little more of the spicy tuna so it looks full, and garnish with chopped green onion.

Salmon Sushi with Green Tea Salt

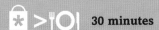 **30 minutes**

The flavors of the salmon, cucumber, and green tea salt are really fresh. The green tea salt will keep for months and is also terrific sprinkled on popcorn.

Makes 18 pieces

2 tablespoons loose green tea

1 sheet nori seaweed, crumbled

1 teaspoon sesame seeds, toasted (see Note, page 34)

1 tablespoon sea salt

1 pound sushi-quality salmon, skin removed

2 tablespoons wasabi paste

1½ cups prepared sushi rice (page 80)

1 hothouse cucumber, sliced into paper-thin circles

1 lemon, cut into small wedges

In a clean coffee grinder or spice mill, buzz the green tea, crumbled nori, and sesame seeds together to a powder. Transfer to a small bowl and mix with the sea salt; set aside. With a sharp knife, slice the salmon into thin, 2-inch-long pieces. Lay a piece of fish in the palm of your hand and spread a very small amount of wasabi on the surface with your finger. Dab your fingers in a little water and grab about 2 tablespoons of sushi rice. While cupping your palm, gently press the rice onto the fish using 2 fingers. Hand-sculpt the sushi into the shape of a small football. Garnish with a paper-thin slice of cucumber draped over the top and a sprinkle of green tea salt. Squirt with a little lemon juice and serve. Awesome!

Yellowtail Sushi with Shiso, Chile, and Sesame

 **30 minutes**

Photo on page 78–79

This recipe went through several incarnations before it came out perfect. The heat of the chile, the sesame, and the minty shiso leaves is amazing. Shiso is one of those ingredients, like lemongrass, that has no real substitute. The leaves taste a little like mint and look like lily pads. If you can't find them in a specialty or Asian market, just buy a few from your neighborhood sushi restaurant. (That's what I do.)

Makes 18 pieces

1 fresh red chile, cut in paper-thin circles
2 tablespoons sesame seeds, toasted (see Note, page 34)
Drop of sesame oil
Drop of low-sodium soy sauce
1 pound sushi-quality yellowtail tuna
2 tablespoons wasabi paste
1½ cups prepared sushi rice (page 80)
18 fresh shiso leaves

In a small bowl, stir together the chile, sesame seeds, sesame oil, and soy sauce. Slice the yellowtail into thin, 2-inch-long strips. Lay a piece of fish in the palm of your hand and spread a very small amount of wasabi on the surface with your finger. Then dampen your fingers in a little water and grab about 2 tablespoons of the sushi rice. Cupping your palm, gently press the rice onto the fish using 2 fingers. Hand-sculpt the sushi into the shape of a small football. Place the sushi on top of a shiso leaf and wrap it around the sides, like a little lettuce cup. Garnish the sushi with a small amount of the red chile mixture using the tip of a chopstick.

Broiled Portobello Sushi with Soy Glaze

 **30 minutes**

Photo on page 78–79

This is a mock broiled eel for that one vegetarian that always shows up. Close your eyes and you won't know the difference.

Makes 18 pieces

¾ cup low-sodium soy sauce

2 tablespoons brown sugar

2 tablespoons sake

1 teaspoon sesame oil

1 garlic clove, smashed

1-inch piece fresh ginger, peeled and minced

3 small portobello mushrooms, cut on the bias in ½-inch slices

1½ cups prepared sushi rice (page 80)

1 sheet nori seaweed, halved and cut in ½-inch strips

2 tablespoons sesame seeds, toasted (see Note, page 34)

Preheat the oven to 400°F. In a small pot, combine the soy sauce, brown sugar, sake, sesame oil, garlic, and ginger over low heat. Swirl the pot around occasionally and cook for about 8 minutes, or until thickened. Lay the mushroom slices in a single layer on a cookie sheet lined with aluminum foil. Brush the portobello mushroom slices with the soy glaze. Bake for 8 to 10 minutes, until the mushrooms brown and shrink slightly.

Dab your fingers in a little water and grab about 2 tablespoons of sushi rice. Gently squeeze it into your palm to make it a compact mound. Put a portobello slice on top of that and wrap it with a band of nori, moistening the ends to seal. Garnish with the sesame seeds.

Sushi Rice

 **30 minutes**

If the rice for this recipe is not perfect, the sushi will be ruined and you'll end up eating out. I strongly recommend investing in a rice cooker. They are relatively inexpensive and the rice comes out perfect every time.

Makes 8 cups

½ cup rice wine vinegar
3 tablespoons sugar
2 teaspoons sea salt
4 cups short-grain white rice
4 cups water

Combine the vinegar, sugar, and sea salt in a small pot over low heat. Stir to dissolve the sugar, remove from heat, and set aside to cool.

Rinse the rice in several changes of fresh water until the water runs clear; then let it drain really well. Put the rice in a rice cooker with the measured water. Turn it on and let it do its thing. When it's done, put the rice in a shallow bowl and drizzle with the vinegar solution. With a spatula, fold the rice to incorporate. Do not stir or mix because the grains will get smashed and the rice will become mushy. This is not what we are going for here. Spread the hot rice out on a cookie sheet and fan to cool it down. The rice should look shiny, be somewhat sticky, and have a nice balance of tart and sweet flavor. Keep the rice covered with a clean dish towel at room temperature until ready to use.

Get a rice cooker. With all that expensive fresh fish lying around, you're going to risk cooking the rice in a pot on the stove? I don't think so."

weekend brunch

Weekend brunch makes me smile. Hanging out in sweat-pants and a T-shirt, with a cup of strong coffee and a plate of perfect scrambled eggs, is an absolute slice of heaven. This chapter has some of my favorite midday fare, from the familiar to the exotic. Whether you favor crepes or scones or Chinese dim sum, you'll find something here to love. If the in-laws are in town, give one of the fancy dishes a try, like Banana-Pecan Pancakes or the Ricotta Tart. If it's just you and your significant other, maybe a batch of Cherry–Poppy Seed Muffins or biscuits with spoon fruit will do the trick. Either way, morning never tasted so good.

Coconut Bread
with Sweet Pineapple Butter

 **1½ hours**

If you're ever in Sydney, Australia, there is a breakfast place in Darlinghurst called bills. The name is simple, and the place serves simply some of the best food I've ever had. When you order coffee, the waiter brings out small plates of warm toasted coconut bread freshly dusted with powered sugar. After one bite, my girlfriend and I decided to go back for breakfast every morning for the rest of our trip. This bread really holds up if you wrap it in plastic or put it in a storage container. You'll still be snacking on it days later.

Serves 8 to 12

Coconut Bread

½ cup (1 stick) unsalted butter, melted, plus
  more for greasing the pan

3 cups all-purpose flour

1 tablespoon baking powder

1 teaspoon salt

1 teaspoon ground cinnamon

1 cup brown sugar, packed

2 eggs, lightly beaten

1 teaspoon vanilla extract

Zest of 1 lemon, finely grated

1½ cups unsweetened coconut milk

1½ cups shredded coconut, toasted (see Note)

Confectioners' sugar, for dusting

Pineapple Butter

1 (8-ounce) can crushed pineapple, drained

1 cup (2 sticks) unsalted butter, softened

Preheat the oven to 375°F. Grease the bottom and sides of a 9 × 5-inch loaf pan with butter. In a large bowl, mix the flour with the baking powder, salt, and cinnamon. In another large bowl, whisk together the melted butter with the brown sugar, eggs, vanilla, and lemon zest. Pour in the coconut milk and whisk together. Pour the wet ingredients into the dry ingredients and fold everything together with a spatula until you have a smooth batter. Gently fold in the shredded coconut until evenly distributed. Pour into the prepared loaf pan and set it on a cookie sheet. Bake for 1 hour to 1 hour 15 minutes, or until a wooden toothpick comes out clean when inserted into the center of the bread. Rotate the pan periodically to ensure even browning. Cool the bread in the pan for 20 minutes or so; then when cool enough to handle, remove the coconut bread to a cutting board and let it cool completely before slicing.

Press the liquid out of the crushed pineapple using the back of a spoon. (If there is too much juice, the fruit will separate from the butter.) In a small bowl, mash the pineapple with the softened butter until well blended. A food processor is a quick alternative to making the compound butter, so use it if you have one. Mound the butter in a small serving bowl. Toast the slices of coconut bread, dust with confectioners' sugar, and serve with the creamy pineapple butter.

Note: *To toast the coconut: Preheat the oven to 350°F. Spread the coconut on a cookie sheet and bake for 15 minutes, stirring it periodically. Toasting will fluff up the coconut and increase its volume (as well as make it taste better).*

Cherry–Poppy Seed Muffins

 **45 minutes**

This is a quick throw-together that should always be in your brunch recipe arsenal. The muffins look and taste great—and you won't have to spend $2.50 in a coffee shop.

Makes 12 muffins

½ cup (1 stick) unsalted butter, melted, plus more for greasing the pan

2 cups all-purpose flour, plus more for dusting the cherries

1 cup sugar, plus more for dusting the top

1 tablespoon baking powder

1 teaspoon salt

1 cup milk

2 eggs, lightly beaten

1 tablespoon poppy seeds

Zest of 1 orange, finely grated

1 cup dried cherries

Preheat the oven to 400°F. Grease a standard 12-cup muffin tin, preferably nonstick, with butter. In a large bowl, mix the flour, sugar, baking powder, and salt together until evenly combined. In another bowl, whisk together the milk and eggs; then add the melted butter, poppy seeds, and orange zest. Make a well in the center of the dry ingredients. Pour the wet ingredients into the well; fold everything together to form a batter. Toss the cherries with some flour to help prevent them from sinking to the bottom of the muffin when baked, and then fold them into the batter. Spoon the batter into the prepared muffin tins, filling them two-thirds full. Dust the surface of the batter with a little sugar to form a crust as the muffins bake. Bake for 20 to 25 minutes, until a wooden toothpick comes out clean when inserted into the center muffin. Place the muffin tin on a cutting board to cool.

Buttermilk Biscuits with Peach and Rosemary Spoon Fruit

 **1½ hours**

Being a kid from South Carolina, I always had fresh biscuits growing up. This recipe is as close to my grandmother's as I could get without having a spiritual adviser. They're big, fat, and light as a cloud, just like I remember them. The peach and rosemary spoon fruit adds a little contemporary twist.

Makes 12 biscuits and 5 cups jam

Rosemary-Peach Jam

12 ripe peaches
1 lemon, halved
6 cups sugar
½ cup freshly squeezed lemon juice
3 fresh rosemary sprigs
1 (1¾-ounce) box powdered fruit pectin
1 tablespoon unsalted butter

Buttermilk Biscuits

4 cups all-purpose flour, plus more for dusting
¼ cup sugar
1 tablespoon salt
1 tablespoon baking powder
2 teaspoons baking soda
1 cup vegetable shortening, cold
2 cups buttermilk, plus more for brushing the biscuits

Blanch the peaches in boiling water for 1 minute. This will not only make them easier to peel but also keep their fresh, summery color. Dump them in a colander and run it under cold water. When cool enough to handle, peel the skins off the peaches with a paring knife, leaving the flesh intact. Cut the peaches in half and discard the pits, and then cut the peaches into chunks; you should have 6 cups. Squeeze the halved lemon over the fruit to prevent it from browning.

Put the peaches in a large stainless steel pot, along with the sugar and the ½ cup of lemon juice. Break the rosemary sprigs in half to release the oils, put them in a piece of cheesecloth, and tie it closed. (When you cook this in the cheesecloth, you'll have the rosemary flavor without the needles.) Toss the rosemary sachet into the pot and bring the fruit to a gentle simmer. Cook and stir with a wooden spoon until the fruit begins to soften and break down to a pulp, about 45 minutes. As it simmers, skim the foam off the top so you have a nice, clear product. Fish out the rosemary bag and stir in the pectin. Turn the heat up and boil for 1 minute, stirring constantly. Remove from the heat, stir in the butter to smooth out the jam, and allow it to cool.

Preheat the oven to 400°F. Sift together the flour, sugar, salt, baking powder, and baking soda. Using 2 forks or a pastry blender, cut in the shortening to coat the pieces with the flour. The mixture should look like coarse crumbs. Make a well in the center and add the buttermilk. Cool your hands by running them under cold water, then use your fingers to fold everything together quickly to form a dough. The shortening in the dough should be as cold as possible. Hands at 98°F. will begin to melt the fat and the biscuits will not rise as high.

Turn the dough out on a floured surface and, again, think cool—don't use the counter next to the pre-heated oven. Roll the dough out to 1 inch thick; then cut out the biscuits using a floured 2-inch round cutter or an inverted glass. Lay the biscuits on an ungreased cookie sheet and brush the tops with buttermilk. Bake for 20 to 25 minutes, until the biscuits have risen and are golden.

Blueberry Scones with Lemon Glaze

 **45 minutes**

These are scones, not stones, the hard, crumbly things you may be used to. Avoid using frozen blueberries because the color bleeds too much into the dough and spoils the look of the scone. This is a side note to all the guys out there. If you bring your woman warm blueberry scones for breakfast in bed, you'll thank me later.

Makes 8 scones

Blueberry Scones

2 cups all-purpose flour, plus more for dusting the blueberries

1 tablespoon baking powder

½ teaspoon salt

2 tablespoons sugar

5 tablespoons unsalted butter, cold, cut in chunks

1 cup heavy cream

1 cup fresh blueberries

Lemon Glaze

½ cup freshly squeezed lemon juice

2 cups confectioners' sugar, sifted

Zest of 1 lemon, finely grated

1 tablespoon unsalted butter

Preheat the oven to 400°F. Sift together the flour, baking powder, salt, and sugar. Using 2 forks or a pastry blender, cut in the butter to coat the pieces with the flour. The mixture should look like coarse crumbs. Make a well in the center and pour in the heavy cream. Fold everything together just to incorporate; do not overwork the dough. Toss the blueberries in some flour to help prevent them from sinking to the bottom of the scone when baked; then fold them into the batter. Take care not to mash or bruise the blueberries because their strong color will bleed into the dough.

Press the dough out on a lightly floured surface into a rectangle about $12 \times 3 \times 1\frac{1}{4}$ inches. Cut the rectangle in half; then cut the pieces in half again, giving you four 3-inch squares. Cut the squares in half on a diagonal to give you the classic triangle shape. Place the scones on an ungreased cookie sheet and bake for 15 to 20 minutes, until beautiful and brown. Let the scones cool a bit before you apply the glaze.

Technically you should make this simple lemon glaze in a double boiler (i.e., over a pot of simmering water with a heatproof bowl set on top) but it's even simpler to zap it in the microwave. Mix the lemon juice and confectioners' sugar together in a microwave-safe bowl. Stir until the sugar dissolves. Add the lemon zest and butter. Nuke it for 30 seconds on high. Whisk the glaze to smooth out any lumps and then drizzle the glaze over the top of the scones. Let it set a minute before serving.

Soft Scrambled Eggs with Smoked Salmon and Avocado

 **20 minutes**

Soft scrambled eggs put a smile on my face in the morning. They are super easy to make and they require very little forethought. I first tasted "real" scrambled eggs while traveling through Paris as a starving college student. Café et des oeufs *was just about all I could afford for breakfast. It was simple, but it was magic.*

Serves 4

8 eggs
3 tablespoons heavy cream
2 tablespoons unsalted butter
Freshly ground black pepper and sea salt
2 avocados, peeled and cut in slices
8 slices smoked salmon
Chopped chives (optional)

Crack the eggs into a bowl. Add the cream and whisk until the eggs look foamy and light. Heat a 10-inch nonstick skillet over medium heat. Melt the butter until it foams; then turn the heat down to low and slowly pour in the eggs. Using a heat-resistant rubber spatula, slowly stir the eggs from the outside of the pan to the center. Once the eggs begin to set, stirring slowly will create large, cloudlike curds. This process takes about 10 minutes. It sounds easy, but perfect scrambled eggs that are soft and custardlike with no brown color are the sign of a really good cook. Season the eggs with a few cranks of black pepper and good salt, like fleur de sel. I like serving these with a few slices of avocado and smoked salmon, maybe a little chopped fresh chives. Once you perfect these, you'll never order eggs at a diner again.

Ricotta Tart with Fresh Tomatoes, Basil, and Black Olives

 **2 hours**

Photo on page 98

This upscale quiche is great for company. Read the section on blind-baking the crust a few times before you get started; it's the trickiest part (but by no means hard). The only special equipment you'll need is a 10½-inch tart pan with a removable bottom. Once you have one of these, you'll use it for a hundred different things, so it's a good investment.

Serves 8

Pastry

1½ cups all-purpose flour, plus more for dusting

½ teaspoon salt

1 teaspoon sugar

½ cup (1 stick) unsalted butter, cold, cut in chunks

1 egg, separated

3 tablespoons ice water, plus more if needed

Ricotta Filling

1 head roasted garlic (see Note)

4 eggs

1 (15-ounce) container ricotta cheese

¼ cup grated Parmigiano-Reggiano cheese

1 teaspoon sea salt

Freshly ground black pepper

Fresh Tomato Salad

4 ripe tomatoes, cut into ¼-inch-thick slices

½ cup pitted and sliced kalamata olives

5 fresh basil leaves, hand-torn

Zest of 1 orange, finely grated

Extra-virgin olive oil

Sea salt and freshly ground black pepper

Using a food processor to make dough is a modern timesaver. The downside is that the blade can really overwork the dough; so be sure to use short bursts of power, not long, sustained ones. Pulse the flour, salt, and sugar together in a food processor. Put in the chunks of butter, a little at a time, and pulse just until the dough resembles cornmeal. Add the egg yolk and the ice water; pulse again for a second just to pull the dough together. Lightly dust the counter with flour. Dump the dough out and briefly knead it by hand into a ball. Again, do not overwork the dough or it will become as tough as shoe leather. Wrap it tightly in plastic and let it rest and chill in the refrigerator for 30 minutes or even overnight. This lets the protein in the flour relax and also firms up the butter particles.

Using a rolling pin, roll the dough out on a lightly floured surface to a 12-inch circle. Carefully roll the dough up onto the pin (this may take a little practice) and lay it inside a 10½-inch tart pan with a removable bottom. Press the edges into the sides of the pan. It is important to press the dough evenly into every nook and corner of the ring, especially the scalloped edges. Fold the excess dough inside to reinforce the rim. Put the tart in the fridge for 15 minutes to relax.

Preheat the oven to 350°F. Prick the bottom of the shell with a fork. Lay a piece of aluminum foil on the bottom of the tart shell and fill it with 1 cup of dried beans. The weight of the beans will keep the pie dough flat so it doesn't bubble when hit with the initial heat. Bake for 30 minutes. Lift out the beans in the foil, return the tart shell to the oven, and bake for another 10 minutes, or until lightly golden.

Beat the egg white with 1 tablespoon of water. Brush the bottom and sides of the pastry with the egg glaze to seal any tiny holes; it also gives the tart a nice sheen. Your tart shell is ready for filling.

Squeeze the roasted garlic cloves out of their skins into a large bowl. Beat in the eggs and ricotta and Parmigiano cheeses; season with salt and pepper. Place the tart shell on a cookie sheet. Pour the egg mixture into the shell, filling it three-quarters of the way. Carefully transfer to the oven and bake for 30 minutes. The tart should still jiggle slightly in the center; it will set up as it cools.

Mix the tomato slices with the olives, basil, and orange zest. Drizzle with a 2-count of oil; season with salt and pepper and fold everything together.

Carefully lift the tart out of the ring and slide the tart off the base and onto a plate. Let the tart cool to room temperature. Cut it into wedges and drizzle with a little olive oil and a few turns of freshly ground black pepper. Spoon some of the tomato salad onto each plate and put a slice of tart on top.

Note: *To roast the garlic, bang the garlic head on the counter to loosen the cloves. Put the separated cloves in a piece of aluminum foil, drizzle with olive oil, and close up the pouch. Bake for 30 minutes (you can bake them with the tart shell). The garlic should be soft.*

Banana-Pecan Pancakes with Maple-Honey Butter

 **45 minutes**

I don't know a man, woman, or child who doesn't love a fluffy stack of pancakes. You can substitute any-thing for the pecans and the banana: strawberry and almond, blueberry and orange, honey and ricotta.

Serves 4

Maple-Honey Butter

1 cup (2 sticks) unsalted butter, softened

¼ cup pure maple syrup

2 tablespoons honey

Banana-Pecan Pancakes

2 cups buttermilk

3 eggs

1 teaspoon pure vanilla extract

2 cups all-purpose flour

3 tablespoons sugar

1½ teaspoons baking powder

1 teaspoon baking soda

¼ teaspoon salt

½ cup pecans, toasted and finely ground (not chopped)

4 tablespoons (½ stick) unsalted butter, melted, plus more for frying

3 bananas, peeled and sliced in ¼-inch circles

In a mixing bowl, mash the softened butter with the maple syrup and honey until well blended. Chill the butter in the fridge for 30 minutes.

Whisk the buttermilk, eggs, and vanilla together until lightly beaten. In another bowl, stir the flour, sugar, baking powder, baking soda, and salt together. Mix the wet ingredients into the dry ingredients to combine. Fold in the pecans and the 4 tablespoons of melted butter; whisk to a smooth batter. Heat a griddle or skillet over medium-low heat and swirl around a little melted butter to keep the pancakes from sticking. Using a ladle or measuring cup, pour the batter into the pan. The trick to perfect round pancakes is pouring all the batter in the same spot and letting it roll out to a complete circle. Cook the pancakes on one side until they set and then lightly press the bananas into the batter. When small bubbles appear on the uncooked surface, flip the pancakes and cook until golden on both sides, about 8 minutes. Keep the pancakes warm in a low (200°F) oven while you make the rest. Slice the maple-honey butter, layer it between the stack of pancakes, and let it melt. Who needs syrup?

Croissant French Toast with Soft Caramel Apples

 30 minutes

I like Granny Smith apples for this particular recipe because of their low water content; they hold up really well when you cook them. Juicy apples, such as McIntosh, are not ideal for this because they fall apart and turn to mush. I developed this recipe at Cafeteria in New York City. The gooey caramel apples are amazing with the croissant French toast. This dish was written up in InStyle *magazine.*

Serves 4

Batter

3 eggs
¼ cup milk
½ teaspoon vanilla extract
Pinch of ground cinnamon

Caramel Apples

½ cup sugar
3 tablespoons unsalted butter
6 Granny Smith apples, peeled, cored, and cut in ½-inch-thick wedges
½ cup maple syrup

3 tablespoons unsalted butter
4 large croissants, split in half lengthwise
Confectioners' sugar, for dusting
Ground cinnamon, for dusting

>>

Make the batter for the French toast by whisking together the eggs, milk, vanilla, and cinnamon until evenly blended. Cover and refrigerate.

Pay close attention while you make the caramel apples. Put the sugar in a large, dry skillet and place it over medium-low heat. Stir constantly with a wooden spoon until the sugar melts and begins to caramelize, about 5 minutes. Be careful; the sugar is *really* hot at this point. Still stirring, add the butter, which will foam a little. Once the sugar and butter become a caramel sauce, fold in the apple wedges. Now, because the apples are cooler than the sugar, the sugar may start to seize and harden, but don't freak out—keep stirring. Once the apples warm up the caramel will smooth out again. When the caramel sauce loosens up and coats the apples, pour in the maple syrup. Give it a stir and simmer for about 10 minutes, until the apples are fork tender. Pull them off the heat and keep them warm.

For the French toast itself, warm the butter in a large nonstick skillet over medium-low heat. You probably will be able to fit only a couple of croissants in the pan at once, so prepare these in batches. Take a croissant half and quickly dredge it in the batter. The key word here is *quickly*; the croissants are very soft and will disintegrate if soaked in the batter. Lay the croissants in the pan, cut side down, and cook for 4 to 5 minutes. Carefully flip them over with a spatula and brown the other side.

The presentation is like a caramel apple sandwich. Put the bottom half of the croissant on a plate; spoon some of the caramel apples on top of that and cover with the top half of the croissant. Dust with confectioners' sugar and cinnamon. This is what I call a breakfast of champions!

Crepes

 ½ hour + resting time

Crepes are one of those brunch dishes that always impress people. They are versatile and a snap to whip out. In this section I've put together a list of some of my favorite ways with the French pancake. All of the recipes are a slight variation of the Basic Crepe Batter, substituting different types of flour, fillings, and techniques. They are all amazing, and after you master the basic crepe batter, you can create your own different recipes. Tapping your inner chef has never been so easy.

Makes 10 (8-inch) crepes

Basic Crepe Batter

1 cup milk
¼ cup cold water
2 eggs
1 cup all-purpose flour
Pinch of salt
3 tablespoons unsalted butter, melted, plus more for sautéing the crepes

Combine the milk, water, eggs, flour, and salt in a blender. Blend on medium speed for 15 seconds, until the batter is smooth and lump-free. Scrape down the sides of the blender and pour in 3 tablespoons of melted butter. Blend it again for a second just to incorporate. Refrigerate the batter for 1 hour to let it rest. If the crepes are made immediately, they have a tendency to be rubbery; when you let the batter rest, the crepes have a better texture and a softer bite.

Put an 8-inch crepe pan or nonstick skillet over medium heat and brush with a little melted butter for added insurance. Pour ¼ cup of batter into the pan and swirl it around so it covers the bottom evenly; pour back any excess. Cook for 30 to 45 seconds, until the crepe batter sets. Lightly bang the edge of the pan with a wooden spoon to loosen the crepe; then flip it and cook another 30 seconds. The art of flipping a crepe in the air takes practice, so make sure no one is looking when you get the first one going. If this intimidates you, use a heatproof rubber spatula to loosen and flip the crepe. The crepes should be pliable, not crisp, and lightly brown. Slide them onto a platter and continue making the crepes until all the batter is used. Cover the stack of crepes with a towel to keep them from drying out.

Variation   Make as usual but . . .

Cocoa Crepes Add 2 tablespoons of cocoa powder and 3 tablespoons of sugar to the blender after you add the flour and salt. Blend and proceed as above.

Honey-Wheat Crepes Substitute ¼ cup whole wheat flour for ¼ cup all-purpose. ¼ cup whole wheat + ¾ cup all-purpose flour = 1 cup. Add 1 tablespoon of honey and 1 tablespoon of sugar to the blender after you add the flour and salt. Blend and proceed as above.

Buckwheat Crepes Substitute ½ cup buckwheat flour for ½ cup all-purpose. ½ cup buckwheat + ½ cup all-purpose flour = 1 cup. Add an additional 2 tablespoons of water to the blender because buckwheat flour is coarser than regular flour. Blend and proceed as above.

"These are amazing! The orange, figs, and ricotta taste like sunshine."

Honey-Wheat Crepes with Sweet Ricotta and Figs

 1½ hours, including resting time   Photo on previous page

Makes 10 (8-inch) crepes

Figs in Simple Syrup

1 cup water

1 orange, sliced in paper-thin circles

2 tablespoons orange liqueur, such as Grand Marnier

2 tablespoons honey

¼ cup sugar

1 cup dried whole figs, split

Crepes

1 recipe Honey-Wheat Crepe Batter (page 105)

1 (15-ounce) container ricotta cheese

¼ cup confectioners' sugar

1 teaspoon cinnamon

1 egg

Melted unsalted butter, for sautéing crepes

Fresh mint leaves, for garnish

Combine the water, orange slices, Grand Marnier, honey, and sugar in a pot and place over medium heat. Add the figs and cook, stirring occasionally, until they reconstitute and the syrup thickens, about 25 minutes.

While the figs cook, make the crepes as directed on page 105.

Stir the ricotta cheese, confectioners' sugar, cinnamon, and egg together in a medium bowl until the mixture smoothes out.

Preheat the oven to 400°F. Forming the crepes for this recipe is kind of like making burritos. Spoon ¼ cup of the ricotta filling along the lower third of the crepe. Fold the bottom edge away from you to just cover the filling, then fold the 2 sides in to the center. Roll the crepe away from you a couple of times to make a package, ending with the seam side down. Put an ovenproof skillet over medium heat. Brush with melted butter. Pan-fry the filled crepes for 2 minutes per side, until crisp and golden. Transfer the pan to the oven and bake for 10 minutes so the egg in the ricotta filling cooks slightly and the cheese sets. Using a spatula, transfer the crepes to a serving plate.

Spoon the figs and oranges with their syrup over the crepes and around the plate. Garnish with fresh mint and wait for the *oohs* and *aahs* from your guests.

Apple, Brie, and Prosciutto Crepes

 1½ **hours, including resting time**

This is basically a classy open-faced pizza.

Makes 10 (8-inch) crepes

1 recipe Basic Crepe Batter (page 104)
1½ cups apple butter
½ pound thinly sliced prosciutto
2 Granny Smith apples, peeled, cored, and thinly sliced
Extra-virgin olive oil
10 ounces Brie cheese, sliced, at room temperature
1 bunch watercress, thick stems discarded
½ bunch fresh chives, cut in 1-inch pieces
Freshly ground black pepper

Make the crepes as indicated in the basic recipe. Preheat the oven to 400°F.

Lay the crepes on a flat surface. Smear the crepes with the apple butter, about 2 tablespoons each. Lay 3 slices of prosciutto in a single layer across the crepes and then add some apple slices. Drizzle a cookie sheet with a little oil and lay 2 crepes side by side on the pan. Bake for 10 to 12 minutes, until crisp like a thin pizza. Take the crepes out of the oven and lay a few slices of the Brie on top so it melts slightly. Add a handful of watercress, some chopped chives, and several turns of freshly ground black pepper. Drizzle with some olive oil before serving.

Goat Cheese Crepe with B.L.T. Salad

 1¾ hours, including resting time

The Green Goddess dressing is also terrific on salad or as a dip for crudités. It will keep for up to a week in the refrigerator stored in a jar or airtight container.

Serves 4–6

Green Goddess Dressing

½ cup sour cream
½ cup mayonnaise
Juice of 1 lemon
2 garlic cloves, coarsely chopped
3 anchovy fillets
1 cup coarsely chopped fresh flat-leaf parsley
2 tablespoons chopped fresh tarragon
2 tablespoons chopped fresh chives
Sea salt and freshly ground black pepper

1 recipe Basic Crepe Batter (page 104)
10 ounces goat cheese, at room temperature
Extra-virgin olive oil

B.L.T. Salad

10 bacon slices
10 plum tomatoes, sliced in ¼-inch circles
½ pound mixed greens
Sea salt and freshly ground black pepper

Puree the dressing ingredients in a blender until creamy and light green. Cover and refrigerate.

Make the crepes as indicated in the basic recipe. Preheat the oven to 400°F. Mash half the goat cheese in a bowl to soften. Drizzle a cookie sheet with a little oil and lay 2 crepes side by side on the pan. Smear the crepes with a thin even layer of the goat cheese. Bake for 10 to 12 minutes, until crisp like a thin pizza.

While the crepes bake, fry the bacon over medium-low heat until crisp on both sides. Put the bacon on a plate lined with paper towels to drain. Tear the bacon into big pieces and put them in a bowl; add the tomatoes and greens. Season with salt and pepper and give everything a toss. Drizzle the salad with ¼ cup of the Green Goddess dressing. Put a handful of salad in the center of each crepe. Garnish with chunks of the remaining goat cheese and several turns of freshly ground black pepper.

Blueberry Blintz

 1½ hours, including resting time

Serves 4–6

1 recipe Basic Crepe Batter (page 104) made with the addition of 1 tablespoon sugar

Cheese Filling

1½ cups cottage cheese

4 ounces cream cheese

3 tablespoons confectioners' sugar

Zest of 1 lemon, finely grated

1 egg

Blueberry Sauce

2 tablespoons butter

2 pints blueberries

¾ cup sugar

1 teaspoon cornstarch

Juice of 1 lemon

Melted unsalted butter, for sautéing blintzes

Confectioners' sugar, for dusting

Make the crepe batter as indicated in the basic recipe, except add 1 tablespoon of sugar to the blender after you add the flour and salt. Make 10 crepes as directed.

In a food processor, combine the cottage cheese, cream cheese, confectioners' sugar, lemon zest, and egg and blend until smooth. Chill the filling to firm it up a bit so it doesn't squirt out of the blintzes.

Combine the butter, blueberries, sugar, cornstarch, and lemon juice in a small pot over medium-high heat. Bring up to a low boil and stir gently until the berries break down and release their natural juices. The consistency should remain a bit chunky. It will thicken up when it cools down slightly.

Preheat the oven to 400°F. Forming the blintzes is kind of like making burritos. Spoon ¼ cup of the cheese filling along the lower third of the crepe. Fold the bottom edge away from you to just cover the filling; then fold the 2 sides in to the center. Roll the crepe away from you a couple of times to make a package, ending with the seam side down. Put an ovenproof skillet over medium heat. Brush with melted butter. Pan-fry the blintzes for 2 minutes per side until crisp and golden. Transfer the pan to the oven and bake for 10 minutes so the egg in the filling cooks slightly and the cheese sets. Using a spatula, transfer the blintzes to serving plates. Spoon the blueberry sauce on top, dust with confectioners' sugar, and serve right away.

Torte of Buckwheat Crepes and Smoked Salmon with Cucumber Vinaigrette

 2 hours, including resting time

This is what I like to call a fancy schmancy dish, but it's so easy to do and you can make it a day ahead. You will need a springform pan.

Serves 8

1 recipe Basic Crepe Batter (page 104) made with ½ cup buckwheat flour, replacing ½ cup of all-purpose flour

2 tablespoons water

1 (8-ounce) package cream cheese, at room temperature

1½ pounds smoked salmon, thinly sliced

1 red onion, finely diced

½ cup coarsely chopped fresh dill

¼ bunch fresh chives, snipped

½ cup capers

Freshly ground black pepper

1 ounce salmon caviar, for garnish

Cucumber Vinaigrette

1 hothouse cucumber, peeled and sliced

¼ bunch fresh flat-leaf parsley, hand-torn

1 tablespoon capers

Juice of 1 lemon

3 tablespoons rice wine vinegar

½ cup extra-virgin olive oil

½ pound mixed greens, for garnish

Make the crepes as indicated in the basic recipe.

Tear off 2 big pieces of plastic wrap and overlap them in the bottom of a 9-inch springform pan, letting the excess hang over the sides of the pan. Put a buckwheat crepe in the bottom of the pan. Using a spoon, smear an even layer of cream cheese on the crepe. It is very important that the cream cheese be at room temperature so it spreads easily and doesn't tear the crepe. Lay several slices of salmon across the crepe in a single layer, completely covering the surface. Put another crepe on top and press it down slightly. Smear the crepe with another layer of cream cheese. Scatter with the diced onion, dill, chives, capers, and freshly ground black pepper. Add another crepe and repeat, alternating the salmon and "stuff" layers until all the crepes are used. You should end up with 5 layers of salmon and 5 "stuff" layers. Top with one last crepe. Save the leftover ingredients to garnish the torte. Fold the plastic wrap up and over to enclose the torte. Weigh the torte down with a small plate and stick it in the refrigerator for several hours or overnight to let it firm up.

Make the cucumber vinaigrette by pureeing all the ingredients together in a blender. Remove the torte from the springform pan and unwrap it. "Ice" the top of the torte with a thin layer of softened cream cheese. Sprinkle with the remaining red onion, dill, chives, and capers and then the salmon caviar. Cut the torte into wedges like a cake. Serve with the mixed greens and cucumber vinaigrette. This is a show-off dish for sure; when I served it in restaurants I charged $14 a slice.

Dim Sum . . . and then some

For me, Chinatown is the most vibrant neighborhood in New York City. The sidewalks are packed with colorful noodle shops, produce stands, fish markets, and amazing authentic Chinese food. After a big night out, my friends and I get together for a big dim sum brunch in Chinatown. A cup of hot tea and a few steamed shrimp and ginger siu mai and I'm good as new.

Dim sum is a traditional Cantonese luncheon of small dumplings, most either steamed or pan-fried. The dumplings themselves are a snap to make and can even be made in advance. When you make them at home you'll be able to taste one of New York's best ethnic foods. You will need a bamboo or metal steamer with stackable layers, which you can pick up for next to nothing at most Asian markets. Dim sum are perfect for company and are great at a cocktail party. As the Chinese say, *Cing Shang* (Enjoy!).

Shrimp and Ginger Siu Mai Dumplings

 **45 minutes**

Makes 36 dumplings

Shrimp Filling

¾ pound shrimp, shelled and deveined

½ pound ground pork

1 green onion, finely chopped

3 garlic cloves, minced

2-inch piece fresh ginger, grated

2 egg whites

2 teaspoons cornstarch

Juice of ½ lemon

1 tablespoon low-sodium soy sauce

1 tablespoon sesame oil

1 tablespoon dry sherry

¼ teaspoon sea salt

¼ teaspoon ground white pepper

1 (10-ounce) package round wonton wrappers

Canola oil, for brushing the steamer

Savoy cabbage, for lining the steamer (optional)

2 green onions, sliced, for garnish

Dipping sauces (page 128)

Pulse the filling ingredients in a food processor until partly smooth but not completely pureed; I like my fillings to have a little texture. Season with salt and pepper.

Hold a wonton wrapper in your hand. Drop 1 tablespoon of the filling onto the center of the wrapper; dipping the spoon in cold water first will make the filling come off easier. Gather the edges of the wrapper up around the filling and squeeze the sides slightly with your fingers. The sides will naturally pleat, leaving the filling slightly exposed. Tap the dumpling on the table so the bottom is flat and it stands upright. Repeat with the remaining wrappers and filling. (You can freeze the leftover filling for 2 or 3 weeks.)

Lightly oil the bottom of a 10-inch bamboo steamer and line it with the whole cabbage leaves. Stand the dumplings in the steamer in a single layer and don't let them touch. You should be able to get 12 siu mai in the steamer at a time. Bring 1 to 2 inches of water to a boil in a wok. Set the bamboo steamer inside the wok, then cover it with the bamboo lid. Steam for 10 to 12 minutes or until the filling feels firm. Garnish with green onions and serve with one of the dipping sauces.

Buddha's Delight

 > 🍴 **45 minutes**

Photo on page 122

Makes 24 dumplings

Vegetable Filling

Sesame oil

2 garlic cloves, minced

1-inch piece fresh ginger, grated

1 leek, well washed and coarsely chopped

1 head baby bok choy, coarsely chopped

½ cup shiitake mushrooms

1 carrot, coarsely chopped

½ bunch fresh cilantro

Sea salt and ground white pepper

2 egg whites

1 tablespoon cornstarch

1 (10-ounce) package round wonton wrappers

1 egg white, lightly beaten

Canola oil, for brushing the steamer

Savoy cabbage, for lining the steamer

Dipping sauces (page 128)

Heat a large skillet over medium heat and coat with a 2-count of sesame oil. Add the garlic and ginger to the pan and stir for 1 minute, until fragrant. Add the leek, bok choy, mushrooms, carrot, and cilantro. Season with salt and pepper. Stir and cook for 5 minutes, until the vegetables soften. Remove from the heat and let the vegetables cool to room temperature. Scrape the vegetable mixture into a food processor; add the egg whites and cornstarch. Pulse the filling until it holds together.

Lay a wonton wrapper on the counter. Brush the surface with the beaten egg white. Drop 1 tablespoon of the mixture onto the center of the wrapper. Fold it in half to make a semicircle and crimp the edges to seal. With the seam side up, tap the bottom lightly on the counter to flatten the base. Repeat with the remaining wrappers and filling.

Lightly oil the bottom of a 10-inch bamboo steamer and line it with whole cabbage leaves. Stand the dumplings in the steamer in a single layer and don't let them touch. You should be able to get 12 dumplings in the steamer at a time. Bring 1 to 2 inches of water to a boil in a wok. Set the bamboo steamer inside the wok; then cover it with the bamboo lid. Steam for 10 to 12 minutes, until the dumplings feel firm. Serve with one of the dipping sauces on page 128. These also work great as hors d'oeuvres for a cocktail party.

Fried Crab Wontons

 **45 minutes**

Photo on page 123

Makes 36 wontons

Crab Filling

Peanut oil, for frying

1-inch piece fresh ginger, grated

1 shallot, finely chopped

½ carrot, finely chopped

12 ounces Dungeness crabmeat, picked through for shells

1 green onion, finely chopped

2 tablespoons finely chopped fresh cilantro

2 tablespoons mayonnaise

Juice of ½ lemon

1 egg white

1 teaspoon cornstarch

¼ teaspoon sea salt

¼ teaspoon ground white pepper

1 (12-ounce) package square wonton wrappers

1 egg white, lightly beaten

Cornstarch, for dusting wontons

Dipping sauces (page 128)

Heat a skillet over medium heat and hit it with a 1-count drizzle of oil. Sauté the ginger, shallot, and carrot for 2 minutes to soften. Put the crabmeat in a mixing bowl and scrape in the ginger mixture. Fold in the remaining ingredients and season with salt and pepper. Be careful not to mash the crabmeat— you want that texture when you bite into the wonton.

Lay a wonton wrapper on a flat surface and brush with the beaten egg white. Drop 1 tablespoon of the crab filling onto the center of the wrapper. Fold the wonton in half, corner to corner, to form a triangle. Press around the filling to knock out any air bubbles and then press the seam together to seal so the filling doesn't seep out when fried. Lightly dust the filled wontons with cornstarch to keep them from sticking and place them on a cookie sheet.

In a wok or heavy pot, heat 2 to 3 inches of peanut oil over medium-high heat. The oil should take about 15 minutes to heat up. Sprinkle a tiny bit of cornstarch in the hot oil; if it sizzles, you are ready to go. If you feel more comfortable checking the temperature of the oil with an instant-read thermometer, it should read 350°F. Drop 5 wontons in the pot, one at a time so they don't stick together, and fry for about 5 minutes, until crisp, turning frequently. Remove with a strainer or slotted spoon and drain on a plate lined with paper towels. Let the oil come back up to temperature and fry the remaining wontons. These are dynamite with all 3 of the sauces on page 128!

* Buddha's Delight

* Fried Crab Wontons

Pork Dumpling Soup
with Chinese Greens

 **45 minutes**

Photo on page 126

These pork dumplings can also be served by themselves without the soup. Just steam them instead of boiling them in the broth. You will have leftover filling, so you can make it once and serve it twice.

Makes 50 dumplings

Pork Filling

¾ pound ground pork

¼ pound shiitake mushrooms, stems removed

½ medium turnip, peeled and grated

1 green onion, finely chopped

2 garlic cloves, minced

½ tablespoon grated fresh ginger

¼ bunch fresh cilantro

1 egg white

2 teaspoons cornstarch

1 tablespoon low-sodium soy sauce

1 tablespoon sesame oil

2 teaspoons dry sherry

¼ teaspoon sea salt

¼ teaspoon ground white pepper

Broth

3 quarts Chicken Stock (page 156)

¼ cup low-sodium soy sauce

2-inch piece ginger, whacked open with the flat side of a knife

4 garlic cloves, smashed

2 green onions, halved

1 dried red chile

1 (12-ounce) package square wonton wrappers

1 egg white, lightly beaten

Cornstarch, for dusting wontons

4 heads baby bok choy, halved lengthwise

¼ pound shiitake mushrooms, stems removed

2 finely chopped green onions, for garnish

Pulse the filling ingredients in a food processor until smooth. Set aside.

In a large pot, simmer the broth ingredients together for 10 minutes to infuse the flavor. Shut it off and cover so you can focus on assembling the dumplings.

Lay a wonton square on a flat surface with one corner facing you. Brush the surface with the beaten egg white and drop 2 teaspoons of the pork filling in the center. Fold the wonton in half, corner to corner, to form a triangle. Press around the filling to knock out any air bubbles; then press the seam together to seal. Brush the 2 side points with beaten egg white. Place your index finger in the center so you have something to press up against; then fold the 2 sides into the center, slightly overlapping, and press the dough against your finger with your thumb to form a tight seal. Lightly dust the filled dumplings with cornstarch to keep them from sticking together and place them on a cookie sheet. When these are folded they look like Pope's hats.

When the dumplings are all filled and folded, strain the soup broth to remove the solids. Bring the soup to a simmer over medium heat. Add the dumplings and boil for 12 minutes. Add the bok choy and shiitakes; continue to simmer for 3 minutes, until tender. Ladle the soup into each bowl and allow 3 dumplings per person. Garnish with green onions and a drizzle of chile oil.

"One of the great things about living in Chinatown is being able to taste the amazing Asian food there. It's like experiencing a different culture in every spoonful."

Sweet Chili Sauce

⋆ **Makes about ¾ cup**

6 tablespoons honey
3 tablespoons red chili paste, such as sambal
2 tablespoons rice wine vinegar

Stir all the ingredients together in a small bowl.

Soy Sauce with Ginger and Shallot

⋆ **Makes almost 1 cup**

½ cup mirin or sake
3 tablespoons low-sodium soy sauce
3 tablespoons rice wine vinegar
1 shallot, cut in paper-thin circles
1-inch piece ginger, peeled and grated

Warm all the ingredients together in a pot for a couple of minutes until heated through. Serve warm or at room temperature.

Chinese Mustard Sauce

★ **Makes 1 cup**

¾ cup Dijon mustard

2 tablespoons Sweet Chile Sauce (see recipe opposite)

1 tablespoon rice wine vinegar

1 teaspoon sesame oil

1 teaspoon finely grated ginger

1 tablespoon hand-shredded fresh cilantro

Blend the mustard with the chile sauce, rice wine vinegar, sesame oil, and ginger until smooth. Let it sit for 1 hour to let the flavors come together. Add the cilantro right before serving.

one-pot wonders

Close your eyes for a second and imagine walking into a house redolent with the aroma of beef bourguignon simmering away on the stove. Hours of slow braising create a dish with a deep red-wine flavor and the rich soft texture of practically melted beef that's perfect and timeless. No wonder it has been around for what seems like forever.

This chapter is dedicated to the classic recipes made in one pot. Beautiful, truly delicious food that's not messed around with; dishes like Risotto with Wild Mushrooms and Peas, New England Clam Chowder, or Chicken Cacciatore, and Lamb Curry. Dishes that are great for company, but also as a Sunday afternoon project that will give you great leftovers to reheat during the week. These are deeply satisfying recipes. You won't soon forget them.

Beef Chili with Ancho, Red Beans, and Chocolate

 **4 hours**

This recipe is a hybrid from different schools of thought. The texture is that of shredded beef, which is authentic Texan, but the flavor is the American Southwest. The dried chilies and the chocolate give this dish an amazing rich, smoky depth. If you're a purist and think adding beans is a sacrilege, leave them out, but they do work really well here. This is truly one of the best dishes I've ever made.

Serves 6 to 12 ★ Makes 3 quarts

2 ancho chiles, seeded and hand-torn into pieces

3 pounds beef shoulder, cut into large cubes

Sea salt and freshly ground black pepper

2 onions, diced

10 garlic cloves, halved

3 canned chipotle peppers in adobo, chopped

1 jalapeño, seeded and chopped

2 tablespoons chili powder

2 tablespoons ground coriander

1 tablespoon ground cumin

1 tablespoon sweet paprika

1 tablespoon dried oregano

¼ teaspoon ground cinnamon

1 teaspoon sugar

1 (28-ounce) can whole tomatoes

2 tablespoons tomato paste

2 (15½-ounce) cans kidney beans, drained

¼ cup cornmeal

1 tablespoon grated unsweetened chocolate

3 cups shredded white Cheddar cheese, for garnish

16 Saltine crackers, for garnish

Making chili is nothing more than mounting layers of flavor and letting them all simmer together. Get in the habit of tasting recipes in stages; this way if something is not quite right, adjustments can be made on the spot.

Toast the ancho chile pieces over low heat in a dry skillet until fragrant, shaking the pan so they don't scorch. Put the chilies in a mini food processor and pulse to a powder. This homemade chile powder will add a smoky depth to the chili. Season the beef shoulder all over with salt and pepper and then put it in a large soup pot. Add enough water to cover by 1 inch, about 3 quarts, and place over medium heat. Bring to a boil and skim off any foam that rises to the surface. Mix in the onions, garlic, chipotles, and jalapeño. Stir in the chili powder, coriander, cumin, paprika, oregano, cinnamon, sugar, and the powdered ancho chilies. Pour the entire can of tomatoes with their liquid into a bowl and hand-crush until chunky; add it to the pot along with the tomato paste. Simmer until the meat is fork-tender and comes apart with no resistance, about 2 hours. As it cooks down, add more water if necessary. When done, take a wooden spoon and beat the chili vigorously so the meat comes apart in shreds.

Add the next layer of flavor by stirring in the beans and cornmeal. Season with salt and pepper and simmer for 1 hour, stirring occasionally. Cover the pot only partially so the steam doesn't get trapped under the lid and drip down into the chili, making it watery. In the last 5 minutes of cooking, stir in the grated chocolate. Garnish each serving with the shredded Cheddar cheese and Saltine crackers.

Beef Bourguignon

 **3 easy hours**

In culinary school, beef bourguignon is one of the first dishes you're taught that truly represents French cuisine. It's basically beef stew with a deep red-wine flavor. The kicker is that it's one of the easiest recipes in this book. Serve this with creamy mashed potatoes and I swear you will feel like Paul Bocuse, and you don't have to go to cooking school.

Serves 6 to 12 ★ **Makes 3 quarts**

Canola oil

4 bacon slices

3½ to 4 pounds beef chuck or round, cut in 2 × 2-inch cubes

Sea salt and freshly ground black pepper

½ cup all-purpose flour

¼ cup Cognac

1 bottle dry red wine, such as Burgundy

1 (14½-ounce) can low-sodium beef broth

2 tablespoons tomato paste

Bouquet garni (1 fresh rosemary sprig, 8 fresh thyme sprigs, 2 bay leaves, tied together with a strip of leek)

4 garlic cloves, chopped

2 cups pearl onions, blanched and peeled

1 pound white mushrooms, stems trimmed

Pinch of sugar

2 tablespoons unsalted butter

Fresh flat-leaf parsley, chopped, for garnish

Place a large Dutch oven over medium heat; drizzle with a ½-count of oil. Fry the bacon until crisp and then remove it to a paper towel; you'll crumble it at the end and use it for garnish. Add the beef to the pot in batches. Fry the cubes in the bacon fat until evenly browned on all sides; turn with tongs. Season with salt and pepper. (Don't skimp on this step—it's key.)

After the meat is browned, put it all back in the pot. Sprinkle the flour over the meat; then stir to make sure the beef is well coated and there are no flour lumps. Pour in the Cognac and stir to scrape up the flavorful bits in the bottom of the pan. Cook and stir to evaporate the alcohol. Pour in the red wine and beef broth; then add the tomato paste and bouquet garni. Stir everything together and bring the pot up to a simmer. Cook until the liquid starts to thicken and has the consistency of a sauce; this should take about 15 minutes. Cover the pot, reduce the heat to low, and simmer for 1 hour.

Uncover the pot and add the garlic, pearl onions, and mushrooms, along with the pinch of sugar to balance out the acid from the red wine. Season with salt and pepper. Turn the heat up slightly and simmer for 30 to 45 minutes longer, until the vegetables and meat are tender. Remove the bouquet garni and then stir in the butter to finish up the sauce. Shower with chopped parsley and the reserved crumbled bacon before serving. Deep and rich flavor!

Osso Buco
with Gremolata

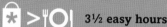 **3½ easy hours**

Simple ingredients with complexity and depth add up to an Italian classic. Oh, and did I mention this is mind-blowing? When purchasing the veal shanks, check that they are pink and smell sweet. The most important step in making Osso Buco is browning the meat. This develops a really rich brown color on the meat and adds a ton of flavor to the base of the sauce. Serve with Soft Polenta (page 244) or Garlic-Chive Mashed Potatoes (page 237). The gremolata is also good on a grilled fish.

Serves 6 to 8 ★ Makes ¼ cup gremolata

Osso Buco

1 cup all-purpose flour

Sea salt and freshly ground black pepper

4 pieces of veal shank for osso buco

Extra-virgin olive oil

3 tablespoons unsalted butter

1 onion, diced

1 celery stalk, diced

2 carrots, diced

1 lemon, zest peeled off in fat strips with a vegetable peeler

4 garlic cloves, minced

2 bay leaves

¼ cup chopped fresh flat-leaf parsley

1 bottle dry red wine, such as Cabernet Sauvignon

1 (14½-ounce) can low-sodium beef broth

1 (28-ounce) can whole tomatoes, hand-crushed

Gremolata

¼ cup pine nuts, toasted

1 anchovy fillet

2 garlic cloves

Zest of 1 orange, finely grated

2 tablespoons chopped fresh flat-leaf parsley

Put the flour in a large shallow platter and season it with a fair amount of salt and pepper. Get in the habit of always tasting your flour; once it coats the veal it is harder to adjust the seasoning. Dredge the veal shanks in the seasoned flour and then tap off the excess (extra flour will burn and make the dish off-tasting). Heat a large Dutch oven over medium heat and hit it with a 3-count drizzle of oil. Add the butter and swirl it around the pan to melt. Sear the veal shanks, turning carefully with tongs, until all sides are a rich brown caramel color. Drizzle with a little more oil if needed. (Do this in batches if the shanks are big and look crowded in the pot.) Remove the browned veal shanks to a side plate. There will be a lot of flavor left over in the bottom of the pot. You're going to use that to create your sauce.

Preheat the oven to 375°F. Using the same pot, sauté the onion, celery, carrots, lemon zest, garlic, bay leaves, and parsley over medium heat. Cook the vegetables down until they start to get some color and develop a deep, rich aroma. Season with salt and pepper; add a little oil if needed. Nestle the veal shanks back in the pot. Pour in the wine and let it simmer down for 20 minutes, until the wine has reduced by half. Reducing is key for intense flavor. Add the beef broth and tomatoes and stir everything together. Cover the pot and put it in the oven. Braise for 1½ hours. Then remove the cover and continue to cook for another 30 minutes. The sauce should be thick and the veal tender and nearly falling off the bone.

For the gremolata, mash the pine nuts, anchovy, and garlic together in a mini chopper or with a mortar and pestle. Fold that into the orange zest and parsley. Scatter the gremolata over the Osso Buco before serving.

Steamed Mussels with Saffron and Tomato

 **45 minutes**

Photo on page 141

Fresh Prince Edward Island mussels are God's gift to an appetizer menu. This dish has worked in every restaurant that I've been involved with and people just love it. If you don't have saffron, it's okay—but the curry is a must. I like serving grilled bread with this for sopping up the delicious broth.

Serves 4 to 6

3 pounds mussels

Extra-virgin olive oil

1 onion, finely chopped

4 garlic cloves, minced

1 tomato, diced

2 bay leaves

Pinch of saffron threads, steeped in
    2 tablespoons hot water

1 teaspoon red pepper flakes

2 teaspoons curry powder

½ cup dry vermouth

Juice of 1 lemon

½ cup Chicken Stock (page 156)

3 tablespoons unsalted butter

Sea salt and freshly ground black pepper

¼ cup finely chopped fresh flat-leaf parsley

Rinse the mussels under cold running water while scrubbing with a vegetable brush. Remove the stringy mussel beards with your thumb and index finger as you wash them. Discard any mussels with broken shells. Heat a 2-count drizzle of oil in a large pot over medium heat. Sauté the onion, garlic, tomato, and bay leaves until the vegetables cook down to a pulp, about 5 minutes. Stir in the "saffron tea," red pepper flakes, and curry. Add the mussels and give everything a good toss. Add the vermouth, lemon juice, and chicken stock; cover the pot and steam over medium-high heat for 10 minutes, until the mussels open. Stir occasionally so that all the mussels are in contact with the heat. Using a slotted spoon, remove the mussels to a warm serving bowl and cover. Pick out the bay leaves. If some of the pieces of vegetables are nestled in the shells, don't sweat it. The sauce itself is a snap. Add the butter to the pot of mussel broth and buzz it down with a handheld blender (you can also transfer it to a regular blender or food processor). What you want is a smooth, yellow sauce. Season with salt and pepper. Pour the sauce over the mussels and shower with parsley before serving. Impressive and uncomplicated.

Risotto with Wild Mushrooms and Peas

 **1½ hours**

This is a great dish to serve on Sunday night when The Sopranos *come on. It's classy and understated. A good way to add more intense mushroom flavor is to throw the mushroom stems in with the chicken stock. Just be sure to brush the mushroom stems first for any loose dirt.*

Serves 6 to 8

Extra-virgin olive oil

1 onion, minced

2 garlic cloves, minced

1 pound assorted mushrooms, such as Portobello, crimini, and chanterelle, stems removed, sliced

Leaves from 3 sprigs fresh thyme

2 tablespoons chopped fresh flat-leaf parsley

2 bay leaves

Sea salt and freshly ground black pepper

2 cups Arborio rice

½ cup dry white wine, such as Pinot Grigio

8 cups Chicken Stock (page 156), heated

1 cup frozen sweet peas, run under cool water to thaw

2 tablespoons unsalted butter

½ cup freshly grated Parmigiano-Reggiano cheese

Fresh flat-leaf parsley, for garnish

Place a large, deep skillet over medium heat and drizzle with a 3-count of oil. Add the onion and garlic, and cook, stirring, for 5 minutes, until soft. Toss in the mushrooms and herbs; cook down until the mushrooms lose their liquid and are lightly browned, about 10 minutes. Season with salt and pepper. Add the rice and stir for a minute or two, until the grains are well coated and opaque. Season again; seasoning in stages makes the rice taste good from the inside out. Stir in the wine and cook a minute to evaporate the alcohol. Pour in 1 cup of the warm stock. Stir with a wooden spoon until the rice has absorbed all the liquid; then add another cup. Keep stirring while adding the stock a cup at a time, allowing the rice to drink it in before adding more. You may not need all the stock. Taste the risotto. It should be slightly firm but creamy—definitely not mushy, but not raw either. Fold in the peas, butter, and Parmigiano cheese. Drizzle with olive oil and garnish with parsley to finish the dish up. Risotto doesn't like to sit around, so serve it immediately.

New England Clam Chowder

 **1 hour**

Good clam chowder starts with really good, fresh clams. It's easy to find them if you live on the coast, but even if you're landlocked in Ohio, you can ask the guy in the seafood department to order them. I use both cherrystones, which are large and meaty, plus smaller littlenecks, which are more delicate and should be cooked only briefly. I don't care for bottled clam juice because of its high sodium content.

Serves 6 to 8

2 dozen littleneck clams
2 dozen cherrystone clams
1 quart water
2 garlic cloves, smashed
2 bay leaves
3 tablespoons unsalted butter
3-ounce piece salt pork
1 celery stalk, diced
1 onion, diced
Leaves from 10 sprigs fresh thyme
¼ cup all-purpose flour
2 Yukon Gold potatoes, peeled and cubed
2 cups heavy cream
1 cup milk
Freshly ground black pepper
Dash of Tabasco sauce
¼ bunch fresh chives, minced

Wash and scrub the clams to get rid of the dirt. Set the littlenecks aside in the refrigerator, and combine the cherrystone clams with the water, garlic, and bay leaves in a large pot. Cover, and steam over medium-high heat until the clams have all popped open, about 15 minutes. Check every 5 minutes to pull out the clams that have opened (some take longer than others), and give the pot a stir. Pull the opened clams out of their shells and chop them roughly. Cover them and set aside. Pour the broth into a big bowl through a strainer that you've lined with cheesecloth, just in case there is leftover sand; set the broth aside. (I once lost the clam chowder world championship thanks to a little sand, so take the extra minute to do this step, because any grit in the base can ruin the entire dish.)

Rinse out the pot and melt the butter over medium heat. Add the salt pork, celery, onion, and thyme. Sauté this together for 5 minutes, until the vegetables soften. Sprinkle the flour into the pot; stir and coat everything well. Gradually pour in the strained clam broth, whisking constantly to break up any lumps of flour. When all the broth is incorporated, fold in the potatoes, and bring to a boil, stirring constantly for about 15 minutes. The soup will start to thicken from the potato starch.

Toss in the littleneck clams and cover the pot to let them steam open, about 5 minutes. Reduce the heat to low and fold in the chopped clams, cream, and milk. Season the soup with many turns of freshly ground black pepper and stir everything together to heat through, but do not let it boil. Serve this in nice big bowls with a dash of Tabasco sauce and some chives. Crusty bread is crucial for dunking. "Wicked good!" as they say in New England. And about that competition—I'll be back next year with my cheesecloth. Judges, you've been warned.

Hot and Sour Noodle Bowl with Prawns and Asparagus

 **1 hour**

I had this dish in a noodle shop in Australia. When I asked the Thai owner for the recipe, he had an odd reaction; out of nowhere this little guy pulls out a karate move and takes a swing at me. In the end, he chased me out of the kitchen with a cleaver, but not before I swiped the recipe. It was worth it. If you are not able to get your hands on kaffir lime leaves, up the lemongrass to 4 stalks. But do make the effort to try to find them in your area or look for them on the Internet; there really is no substitute for their amazing flavor.

Serves 4 to 6

24 large shrimp (about 2 to 2½ pounds), tails on

3 quarts Chicken Stock (page 156)

2-inch piece fresh ginger, whacked open with the flat side of a knife

2 stalks lemongrass, white part only, whacked open with the flat side of a knife

6 kaffir lime leaves

2 tablespoons brown sugar

1 tablespoon Thai fish sauce (nam pla)

2 teaspoons chili paste, such as sambal

Juice of 1 lime

1 bunch asparagus, bottoms removed, split lengthwise

¼ pound shiitake mushrooms, stems removed, sliced

1 (1½-ounce) package cellophane noodles, blanched for 2 minutes in salted boiling water

Chopped peanuts, fresh cilantro leaves, and fresh mint leaves, for garnish

Peel and devein the shrimp. Set the shrimp aside and put the shrimp shells in a soup pot with the chicken stock. Add the ginger, lemongrass, and lime leaves to the pot; this is the flavor base. Stir in the brown sugar, fish sauce, chili paste, and lime juice. Let the soup simmer for 10 minutes, until your kitchen smells amazing. Strain the broth into another pot to remove the solid pieces; then add the shrimp, asparagus, and mushrooms. Poach in the simmering soup for 5 minutes. Divide the cooked noodles among dinner bowls, ladle the soup on top, and finish with the peanuts, cilantro, and mint. Banging, baby!

Chicken Cacciatore

 **2 hours**

Photo on page 150

Chicken Cacciatore is a dish that time has forgotten. It's simple, rustic, and truly Italian, and my buddy Frankie DeCarlo likes it, too. I would serve this with Soft Polenta (page 244). If cutting up a chicken intimidates you, buy precut pieces or have the guy at the meat counter do it for you—that's his job, right?

Serves 6

6 red bell peppers

Extra-virgin olive oil

Sea salt and freshly ground black pepper

1½ cups all-purpose flour

2 tablespoons garlic powder

1 tablespoon dried oregano

1 egg

2 cups milk

1 (3½-pound) whole chicken, cut into 8 pieces

6 garlic cloves, halved lengthwise

1 onion, sliced thin

2 ripe tomatoes, coarsely chopped

½ lemon, sliced in paper-thin circles

3 anchovy fillets

1 tablespoon capers

1 teaspoon red pepper flakes

½ bunch fresh basil, hand-torn (¼ bunch to flavor the base, ¼ bunch to finish the dish)

1 cup dry white wine

Start by preparing the peppers because they will take the longest. Preheat the broiler. Pull out the cores of the red peppers; then halve them lengthwise and remove the ribs and seeds. Toss the peppers with a little olive oil, salt, and pepper. Place them on a cookie sheet, skin side up, and broil for 10 minutes, until really charred and blistered. Put the peppers into a bowl, cover with plastic wrap, and steam for about 10 minutes to loosen the skins. Peel the red peppers and roughly chop them into chunks; set aside.

Season the flour with the garlic powder, dried oregano, and a fair amount of salt and pepper. Whisk the egg and milk together in a shallow bowl. Dredge the chicken pieces in the flour and tap off the excess. Dip each piece in the egg wash to coat and then dredge with the flour again. Place a Dutch oven over medium heat and pour in about ¼ inch of oil. Pan-fry the chicken in batches, skin side down, until crisp, about 8 minutes. Turn the chicken over and brown the other side about 10 minutes longer. Remove the chicken to a side plate, pour out the oil, and clean out the pot.

Put the pot back on the stove and coat with ¼ cup of oil. Add the garlic, onion, tomatoes, lemon slices, anchovies, capers, red pepper flakes, half the roasted red peppers, and half the basil. Season with salt and pepper. This part of the recipe is going to be your base. What we are looking for is a fragrant vegetable pulp, so simmer for about 20 minutes, stirring often, until everything breaks down. (I know it's good, but keep your spoon out of it.)

Add the remaining roasted peppers and the remaining basil. Tuck the chicken into the stewed peppers and pour in the wine. Turn the heat down to low, cover, and simmer for 20 minutes, until the chicken is cooked.

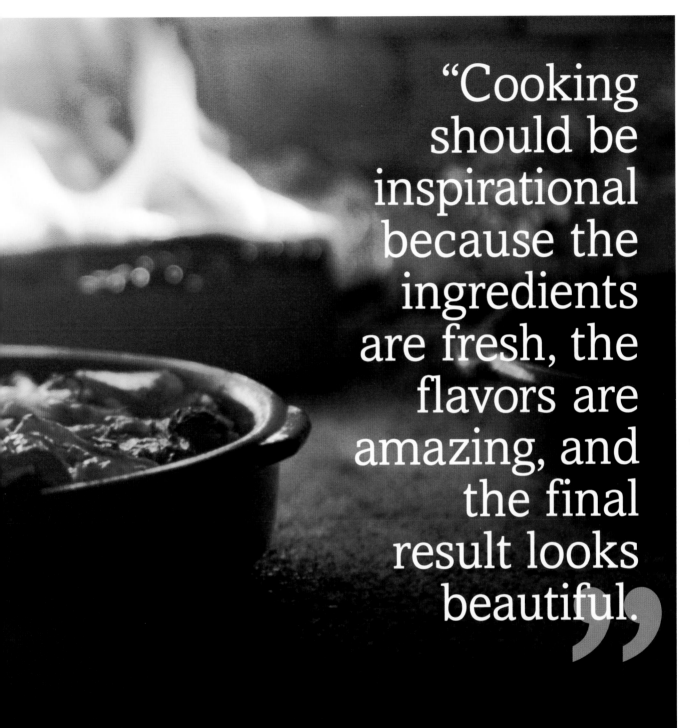

"Cooking should be inspirational because the ingredients are fresh, the flavors are amazing, and the final result looks beautiful."

Maine Lobster Boil with Drawn Lemon Butter

 **40 minutes**

This is an easy recipe for a late summer backyard feast. Steamed lobster, lemony butter, and a few cold beers: That's love. Special equipment needed: kitchen shears, tongs, crackers, bibs, and a napkin to wipe your chin.

Serves 4

Lobsters

1 gallon water

½ bunch fresh thyme

4 bay leaves

2 lemons, halved

4 live lobsters, about 2 pounds each (see Note)

Drawn Lemon Butter

1 cup (2 sticks) unsalted butter

Juice of 1 lemon

Make a tasty cooking broth by combining the water, thyme, and bay leaves in a very big pot. Squeeze the lemon juice into the water and then drop in the empty rinds. Bring the pot up to a high boil. Plunge the lobsters into the boiling water, cover, and boil for 15 minutes. The lobster shells will be bright red and the tails will be curled when they are done.

While the lobsters cook, make the lemon butter. Heat the butter in a small pot over low heat. Warm it up gently so the milk solids begin to cook and sink to the bottom of the pot. Keep a close watch because once the milk solids collect and fall, they burn really easily. Strain the clear butter into a small serving cup, leaving the solids behind, and give a squeeze of lemon juice.

Note*: For some, the humane factor comes into cooking live lobsters. If you stick them in the freezer for 10 minutes they will squirm less as you dunk them in boiling water. If you prefer to take a knife and do a quick jab to the lobster's spinal cord as the means to its end, go right ahead.*

Lamb Curry

 >¶◯| **2 hours**

For me, commercially produced curry power tastes just that: commercial. You would never find pre-pared curry powder in an Indian restaurant, and because the spices are combined fresh, the flavors are robust and explosive. If you like a light curry flavor, use half the spice mix. If you like a spicy curry—use it all. I won't be mad at ya. Serve the lamb curry with Perfect Steamed Jasmine Rice (page 240) or basmati rice. This is Bombay the right way.

Serves 6 to 12 ✳ Makes 3 quarts ✳ ¾ cup spice mix

Spice Mix

2 tablespoons black mustard seeds

2 teaspoons coriander seeds

2 teaspoons ground cardamom

2 teaspoons cumin seeds

½ teaspoon whole black peppercorns

2 tablespoons garam masala

2 teaspoons turmeric

2 teaspoons red pepper flakes

Cinnamon stick

Curry

3 pounds boneless leg of lamb, trimmed of excess fat, cut into 1-inch cubes

Sea salt and freshly ground black pepper

Canola oil

1 onion, finely chopped

2 garlic cloves, minced

1 tablespoon minced fresh ginger

2 bay leaves

3 cups Chicken Stock (page 156)

1 cup tomato puree

Juice of ½ lemon

2 Yukon Gold potatoes, peeled, cut into 1-inch cubes

½ cup raisins

½ cup blanched almonds

1 cup plain yogurt

Chopped fresh cilantro and fresh mint, for garnish

>>

Make the spice mix by toasting the spices in a dry skillet over low heat. Shake the pan so they don't scorch; when they smell fragrant, not burnt, they're done. Remove and set aside the cinnamon stick; it will go in the stew whole. Transfer the rest of the toasted spices to a spice mill or clean coffee grinder, and grind them to a fine powder.

Season the lamb generously with salt and pepper. Heat a 3-count drizzle of oil in a large Dutch oven over medium heat. Brown the lamb cubes on all sides, turning with tongs, and then remove to a platter. Do this in batches if the pan looks crowded. In the same pot, cook the onion, garlic, ginger, bay leaves, and all the toasted spices in the lamb drippings, stirring occasionally until fragrant, about 3 minutes.

Return the lamb to the pan, add the cinnamon stick, and pour in the chicken stock, tomato puree, and lemon juice. Bring to a simmer, cover, and cook over low heat for 45 minutes. Add the potatoes, raisins, and almonds; season with salt. Stir everything together, cover, and cook another 30 minutes, stirring occasionally. Turn the heat off and mix in the yogurt. Garnish with cilantro and mint before serving. Intense!

Chicken Stock

* **Makes 2 quarts**
* **From grocery bag to plate: 1 hour**

Always have this on hand.

Extra-virgin olive oil
2 carrots, cut into large chunks
2 celery stalks, cut into large chunks
1 onion, halved
1 turnip, halved
1 head of garlic, halved

Chicken bones
3 quarts cold water
¼ bunch fresh flat-leaf parsley
¼ bunch fresh thyme
2 bay leaves

Coat the bottom of a large stockpot with olive oil and place over medium heat. Add the vegetables and sauté for 3 minutes. Add the chicken bones, water, and herbs; simmer for 1 hour, uncovered. Strain the stock to remove the solids and cool to room temperature before storing in the refrigerator. Or chill it down over ice.

Stir-Fried Beef with Tangerines, Green Beans, and Chiles

 **1 hour**

Slicing the beef paper-thin when stir-frying will get the meat nice and crispy, so make sure your knife is sharp. If tangerines are not in season, oranges make a fine substitute and no one will be the wiser. The only weird ingredient is the black Chinese vinegar. It has a sweet, malted flavor that is very traditional in Chinese cooking. If you're a purist about Chinese food, the black vinegar will be worth the trip to an Asian market. If you can't find it, I'm not going to tell anyone if you substitute balsamic vinegar.

Serves 6

Marinade

1 egg white

½ teaspoon sesame oil

1 teaspoon Chinese five spice powder

1 tablespoon cornstarch

Sea salt and ground white pepper

1 pound boneless beef top round, sliced paper-thin against the grain

3 cups peanut oil

1 tangerine, unpeeled, sliced in paper-thin circles

2 tablespoons cornstarch

1-inch piece fresh ginger, minced

4 garlic cloves, minced

2 green onions, minced

4 dried red chiles

¾ pound green beans, halved on the bias

¼ cup Chicken Stock (page 156)

2 tablespoons low-sodium soy sauce

1 tablespoon Chinese black vinegar or balsamic

1 tablespoon sugar

2 tablespoons toasted sesame seeds, for garnish (see Note, page 34)

>>

157

In a mixing bowl, whisk together the egg white, sesame oil, five spice powder, and cornstarch; season with salt and pepper. Add the beef, toss to coat in the marinade, and stick it in the refrigerator for 30 minutes. In the meantime . . .

Pour the peanut oil into a wok and place over high heat. Heat the oil to 350°F.; this will take about 15 minutes. Toss the tangerine slices with 1 tablespoon of the cornstarch. When the oil is smoking hot, quickly fry the tangerine slices for about 4 minutes. Frying the tangerine first removes the bitterness from the skin and the slices become crispy so you can eat them whole. Carefully remove the tangerine slices with a strainer to drain on a paper-towel-lined platter; their shape should remain intact.

Bring the oil back up to the smoking point and add half of the beef. (If you fry all the meat at once the oil temperature will drop and the beef will stew instead of crisp.) Fry for 2 minutes and then remove to a paper towel to drain; repeat with the remaining beef. Very carefully drain all but ¼ cup of the hot oil into a heat-proof container. Stir-fry the ginger, garlic, green onions, and chiles in the remaining oil until they perfume. Add the green beans; season with salt and pepper. Mix the chicken stock with the remaining tablespoon of cornstarch and add it to the wok. Add the soy sauce, vinegar, and sugar. Simmer until the sauce is thick and the beans are tender, about 10 minutes. Return the beef and tangerines to the pan and coat. Scatter the sesame seeds on top. Serve with steamed rice.

Arroz con Pollo
with Salsa Verde

 **2½ hours**

In translation, arroz con pollo *simply means "rice with chicken." When I was the chef at Cafeteria, the Latin American cooks made this dish for our staff meal just about every day. Its truly authentic flavors are homey and satisfying. I prefer using whole canned tomatoes and crushing them by hand because I have more control of the texture; plus the flavor is a lot better than chopped canned tomatoes.*

Serves 6

Arroz con Pollo

1 tablespoon ground cumin

1 tablespoon dried oregano

2 teaspoons sweet paprika

1 teaspoon cayenne

1 teaspoon ground cinnamon

Sea salt and freshly ground black pepper

Canola oil

1 whole chicken, about 3 pounds, cut into 10 pieces

1 pound chorizo sausages, cut into 1-inch chunks

1 Spanish onion, diced

2 garlic cloves, minced

1 red bell pepper, seeded and chopped

2 bay leaves

2 cups long-grain white rice

1 (28-ounce) can whole tomatoes

1 quart Chicken Stock (page 156)

1 cup pimiento-stuffed green olives

Salsa Verde

1 jalapeño pepper, minced

½ bunch fresh cilantro

¼ cup blanched almonds, toasted

½ cup extra-virgin olive oil

Juice of 1 lime

½ teaspoon salt

In a bowl, mix the together the cumin, oregano, paprika, cayenne, and cinnamon; season with salt and pepper. Hit the spice mix with a 3-count drizzle of oil—just enough to moisten—and mash everything together with a fork to create a smooth paste. Rinse the chicken pieces and pat them dry. Rub the chicken with the spice paste and let it sit for 20 minutes to develop the flavor. While the chicken is marinating, cook the chorizo.

Place a large, wide Dutch oven over medium heat and hit it with a ½-count of oil. Toss in the chorizo and fry it until it renders its fat and gets crispy. Remove the chorizo with a slotted spoon and drain it on a paper-towel-lined platter.

Preheat the oven to 350°F.

Brown the chicken in the chorizo fat, skin side down. Depending on the pot you're using, you may have to do this in batches so you don't overcrowd things. When you can move the chicken around without the skin sticking to the bottom of the pan, flip it over and brown the other side. This whole process should take about 15 minutes. Take the chicken out of the pan and set it aside. Make a sofrito by adding the onion, garlic, bell pepper, and bay leaves to the pot; sauté until the vegetables are very soft and almost dissolved, about 10 minutes. Fold in the rice so the grains are well coated with all that flavor. Pour the entire can of tomatoes with the liquid into a bowl and hand-crush until chunky; add it to the pot along with the chicken stock. Season with salt and pepper. Return the chorizo and chicken to the pan. Bring the mixture to a boil and let it simmer for 5 minutes. Cover and transfer the pot to the oven. Bake for 25 minutes or until the chicken is done and the rice is tender and has absorbed the liquid. In the last 5 minutes of cooking, fold in the olives.

To prepare the Salsa Verde: With a mortar and pestle or food processor, mash or pulse all the ingredients together to form a chunky paste. Garnish the Arroz con Pollo with Salsa Verde before serving.

food for the great outdoors

As far as I'm concerned, backyard cookouts are the best thing about summer. The grill is cranked up high, the drinks are cold, and everyone is enjoying themselves. Throwing a great party with amazing low-maintenance food only makes the event that much better, because you can actually enjoy yourself. This chapter is loaded with classic techniques and a few fresh, modern flavors that will keep your backyard, pool, or, in my case, rooftop, packed all summer.

Chinese Spareribs No. 5 with Teriyaki Glaze

 **2 hours**

New York City has a Chinese takeout restaurant on every corner and oddly enough they all seem to have the same menu. Maybe it all comes out of the same kitchen—who knows? What I do know is that Chinese spareribs are one of my favorite junk foods on the planet. This is my variation of the classic Chinese spareribs No. 5. Be warned, they are really addictive. When preparing ribs, slower and longer is always better.

Serves 8 to 10 ★ Makes 1½ cups glaze

2 racks pork spareribs, 4 pounds each, trimmed of excess fat
½ cup Chinese five spice powder
Sea salt and freshly ground black pepper
2 tablespoons sesame seeds, for garnish
Chopped fresh cilantro and green onion, for garnish

Teriyaki Glaze

1 cup low-sodium soy sauce
1 cup grapefruit juice
¼ cup hoisin sauce
¼ cup ketchup
3 tablespoons rice wine vinegar
¼ cup brown sugar
1 fresh red chile, halved
5 garlic cloves, halved
2-inch piece fresh ginger, whacked open with the flat side of a knife

Dust the ribs all over with the five spice powder; season generously with salt and pepper. Prepare a gas or charcoal grill with a cover. You want to cook the ribs slowly over indirect heat for an hour or so first and then crisp them up right before serving. If using a charcoal grill, start with about 15 briquettes, just enough to maintain a low heat. Mound the hot coals on one side of the grill and slow-roast the ribs on the opposite side, away from the heat. If you are using a gas grill, the top warming rack is perfect for this indirect slow-roasting method. Either way, make sure the grill is covered and the temperature is low; slower and longer is always better. Cook the ribs for 1½ hours, turning every 30 minutes. At the end, the pork will pull away from the bone and you will see about ½ inch of the bone showing. While the ribs are working, step into the kitchen to make the teriyaki glaze.

In a pot, combine the soy sauce, grapefruit juice, hoisin sauce, ketchup, rice wine vinegar, brown sugar, chile, garlic, and ginger over medium heat. Bring to a slow simmer and cook, stirring, until thickened, about 20 minutes.

Take the cover off the grill and stoke up the fire with more briquettes until medium-hot. Baste the ribs with the teriyaki sauce and grill uncovered for 15 minutes. A side note: Now is *not* the time to get a beer; these go from perfectly crisp to perfectly burnt in the blink of an eye. Turn them over, baste again, and grill the other side for 15 minutes. Separate the ribs with a cleaver or sharp knife, pile them on a platter, and pour on the remaining sauce. Sprinkle with the sesame seeds, chopped cilantro, and green onion before serving.

Oven Variation

Preheat the oven to 300°F. Arrange the ribs in a single layer in a roasting pan and slow-roast for 2½ hours. In the last 30 minutes of cooking, baste the ribs with the teriyaki sauce. When the ribs are done, the pork will pull away from the bone and you will see about ½ inch of bone showing. Just before you're ready to eat, baste the ribs with the teriyaki sauce again and turn the oven up to 500°F. Cook for 10 minutes to make the spareribs a nice crusty brown.

Pork Roast
with Cabbage, Apple,
and Bacon Slaw

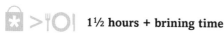 **1½ hours + brining time**

*Pork roasts are perfect for picnics. One dish and you're set—all you need to do is slice it and serve it
(with a dollop of slaw on the side, of course). Leftovers, if there are any, make a dynamite wrap the
next day. Brine the pork roast the morning you plan to serve it for dinner. The meat needs a good
6 hours to break down. Do not let it soak overnight or the pork gets too mushy. The result is the most
tender pork on the planet. Serve with Corn Roasted in Its Own Jacket (page 265) if you wish.*

Serves 8 to 12 ★ Makes 6 cups slaw

Pork Roast

1 gallon water

1 cup brown sugar, packed

1 cup sea salt

1 teaspoon black peppercorns

2 bay leaves

1 shallot, sliced

½ bunch fresh thyme sprigs
(half for the brine, half for the roast)

5½-pound center-section boneless
pork loin roast, tied

Sea salt and freshly ground black pepper

Canola oil

Slaw

6 bacon slices

½ head cabbage, such as napa or
Savoy, shredded

2 McIntosh apples, unpeeled, halved, cored,
and sliced thin

Juice of 1 lemon

½ red onion, sliced thin

½ bunch fresh chives, cut in 1-inch pieces

¼ cup grainy mustard

¼ cup mayonnaise

Pinch of sugar

2 tablespoons cider vinegar

Combine the water, brown sugar, sea salt, peppercorns, bay leaves, shallot, and half the thyme in a large pot or plastic bag. Give it a stir to dissolve the sugar and salt. Submerge the pork in the brine, close it up, and put it in the refrigerator for 6 hours to tenderize and sweeten the meat.

Preheat the oven to 400°F. Remove the pork from the brine and pat it dry with paper towels. Season the pork generously with salt and pepper. Set a large roasting pan over 2 burners and turn the heat to medium-high. Pour a 3-count of oil into the pan and get it nice and hot. Sear the pork on all sides, turning it so the roast browns evenly. Scatter the remaining thyme sprigs on and around the pork and transfer the roast to the oven. Roast for 50 minutes or until an instant-read thermometer reads 155°F. when inserted into the thickest part of the meat. The center of the meat should be a rosy pink. While the meat roasts, you have got plenty of time to bang out the slaw.

Fry the bacon in a skillet over low heat until crisp and then drain on paper towels. Combine the rest of the slaw ingredients in a large bowl. Fold the ingredients together until everything is coated and creamy; season with salt and pepper. Remove the pork from the oven and let it rest for 10 minutes before slicing it thin. Serve the pork with the apple slaw and crumble the bacon on top before serving.

Grilled Steak Sandwich with Portobellos, Grilled Onions, and Fontina

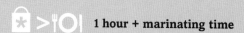 **1 hour + marinating time**

The key to success with this sandwich is knowing which way to slice the flank steak: against the grain of the muscle fibers. Hey, Philly never had it so good.

Serves 4 ✴ Makes 2 cups mayonnaise

Steak

1 head garlic
2 shallots
Needles from 2 rosemary sprigs
1 bay leaf
1 cup plus 2 tablespoons extra-virgin olive oil
Sea salt and freshly ground black pepper
1½ pounds flank steak, about ¾ inch thick

Arugula Mayonnaise

¾ cup mayonnaise
Juice of ½ lemon
2 tablespoons fresh or prepared grated horseradish
2 bunches coarsely chopped arugula
Sea salt and freshly ground black pepper

Everything Else

4 portobello mushrooms, stems removed
1 red onion, sliced
2 tablespoons balsamic vinegar
¼ cup extra-virgin olive oil
Sea salt and freshly ground black pepper
1 loaf ciabatta bread, split horizontally
¼ pound fontina cheese slices
1 bunch arugula

Preheat the oven to 350°F. Roasting garlic and shallots brings out their incredible sweetness and only adds one quick cooking step. Peel off the outer layer of the garlic and shallot skins. Smash them open with the flat side of a knife to break up the cloves. Rip off a large piece of heavy-duty aluminum foil and put the garlic and shallots in the center. Toss in the rosemary and bay leaf and moisten with 2 tablespoons of the oil and 1 tablespoon of water. Wrap up the aluminum pouch, making sure it is sealed tightly so none of the liquid seeps out. Put the pouch in the oven for 20 minutes to steam and soften the garlic and shallots. Unwrap the aluminum and carefully pour any juices into a food processor. Peel the garlic cloves and shallots and toss them into the food processor along with the remaining 1 cup of oil. Season with salt and pepper and pulse until the mixture is well blended. Lay the steak in a shallow platter and pour the flavored oil on top. Cover and refrigerate for at least 2 hours or up to overnight, turning the steak over occasionally so both sides feel the love of the oil.

To make the arugula mayonnaise, combine the mayo, lemon juice, horseradish, and arugula in a food processor. Turn the machine on for 1 minute to combine all the ingredients; the mayo will have a bright green color. Season with salt and pepper, cover, and pop it in the refrigerator.

Lay the mushrooms and onion slices in a shallow platter, drizzle with the vinegar and oil, and season with salt and pepper. Try not to break up the onion slices into rings, they are easier to grill as slices. Take the steak, mushrooms, and onions outside because we're about to make some magic.

Preheat your grill until it's very hot. Take a few paper towels and fold them several times to make a thick square. Blot a small amount of oil on the paper towel and then carefully and quickly wipe the hot grates of the grill. This will create a nonstick grilling surface. Grill the steak for 7 minutes per side for medium-rare. Remove the steak to a cutting board and let it rest for 10 minutes. While the steak rests, grill the mushrooms and onions for about 5 minutes per side so they have a nice char. Brush the cut sides of the ciabatta bread with a little bit of oil and grill for a minute to toast. Slice the mushrooms, separate the onion slices into rings, and slice the steak, paper-thin, against the grain.

Now you are ready to put this awesome sandwich together. To assemble, spread both sides of the bread with the arugula mayonnaise. Lay several slices of flank steak on the bottom bread half and mound with mushrooms and onions. Cover with a couple of slices of fontina cheese and cap it all with the top half of bread. Slice the loaf into 4 sandwiches. Garnish with arugula and serve. It's a beautiful thing.

Horseradish Burgers with Havarti and Tomato Remoulade

 **1 hour**

Photo on page 174–75

Anyone can grill a piece of meat and call it a hamburger, but creating a masterpiece takes a little bit of imagination. Mixing horseradish and chives into burgers will transform you into the Greek god of grilling right before your friends' eyes.

Serves 8 ★ Makes 2¼ cups remoulade

Tomato Remoulade

2 cups mayonnaise

1 tablespoon tomato paste

2 tablespoons capers, drained

1 garlic clove, coarsely chopped

1½ teaspoons Dijon mustard

1 anchovy fillet, coarsely chopped

2 tablespoons chopped fresh parsley

1 tablespoon chopped fresh tarragon

Dash of Tabasco sauce

1 dill pickle, coarsely chopped

Sea salt and freshly ground black pepper

Burgers

2 pounds ground chuck

¼ cup grated fresh or prepared horseradish

½ bunch fresh chives, minced

Sea salt and freshly ground black pepper

Canola oil

16 slices Havarti cheese

8 large hamburger buns, split

Cooked bacon, lettuce, sliced tomato, and onion, for garnish

In a food processor, combine all the ingredients for the remoulade. Pulse a few times to combine. Cover the remoulade and pop it in the fridge while you make the burgers.

Put the beef in a large mixing bowl. Use a rubber spatula to fold in the horseradish and chives; season with salt and pepper. Hand-form the meat into 8 burgers, cover them, and set them aside in the fridge while you prepare your grill.

Preheat a gas or charcoal grill and get it very hot. Burgers stick to a cold grill, so it's important that you give the grill plenty of time to heat. Here is a restaurant tip to keep food from sticking to your grill: Take a few paper towels and fold them several times to make a thick square. Blot a small amount of oil on the paper towel; then carefully and quickly wipe the hot grates of the grill. This will create a nonstick grilling surface. Grill the burgers for 8 minutes per side for medium; 7 minutes if you like your meat rare. If you like well done, I can't help you.

When the burgers are just about cooked, put a couple of slices of cheese on top of each and cover the grill for 1 minute to melt the cheese. Remove the burgers to a clean side plate so you have enough room to toast the buns.

Rub the grill rack with the same paper towel as before to clean off the small charred pieces; then toast the hamburger buns cut side down for 1 minute. Serve the burgers with the tomato remoulade and any garnish you like, such as bacon, lettuce, sliced tomato, or onion.

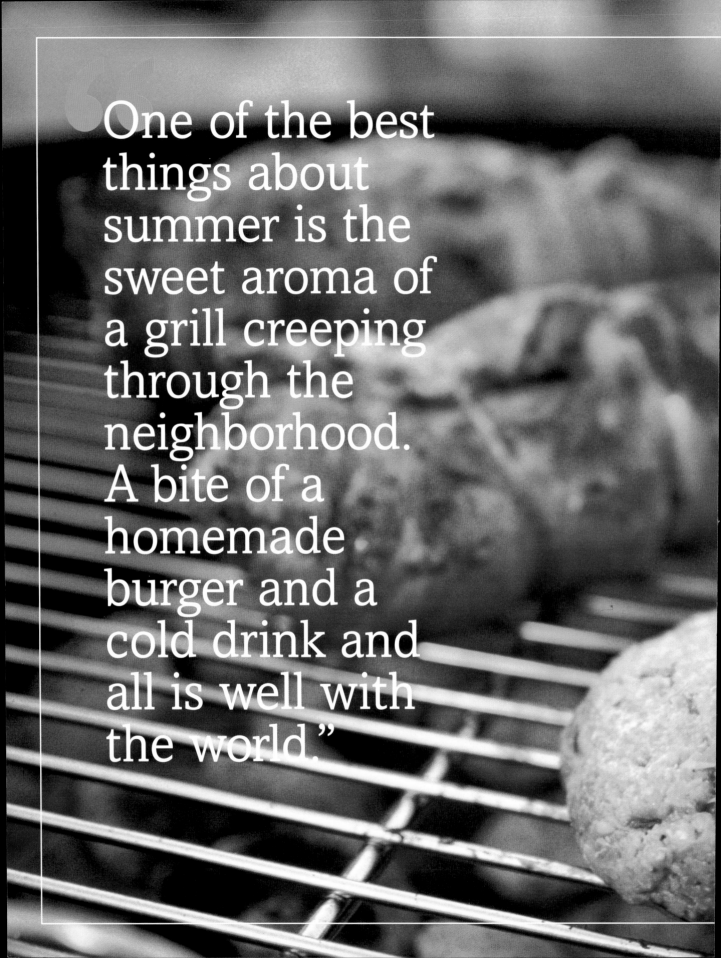

"One of the best things about summer is the sweet aroma of a grill creeping through the neighborhood. A bite of a homemade burger and a cold drink and all is well with the world."

Spiced Leg of Lamb with Fig Caponata and Harissa

 2 hours + resting time

Photo on page 174

The foods from North Africa and the Middle East truly have some of the deepest flavors I've ever tasted. Don't be daunted by the length of the recipe: This dish is not at all difficult to throw down, and the results are well worth the long shopping list. The Harissa sauce can be made a day ahead and the caponata is also good by itself or as a side dish.

Serves 6 to 8

Harissa Sauce

2 red bell peppers

1 teaspoon cumin seed

1 teaspoon coriander seed

1 teaspoon caraway seed

2 garlic cloves

2 small fresh red chiles, chopped

1 teaspoon sea salt

3 tablespoons extra-virgin olive oil

Fig Caponata

½ cup extra-virgin olive oil

3 anchovy fillets, coarsely chopped

1 teaspoon red pepper flakes

1 large Italian eggplant, cubed

2 tomatoes, halved and seeds squeezed out, coarsely chopped

1 onion, diced

3 garlic cloves, minced

3 tablespoons capers, drained

¼ cup raisins

¼ cup pine nuts

2 tablespoons balsamic vinegar

1 tablespoon sugar

½ bunch fresh basil, hand-torn

Sea salt and freshly ground black pepper

8 fresh Mission figs, halved

Spiced Leg of Lamb

5- to 7-pound leg of lamb, boned, butterflied, and surface fat removed

½ cup plain yogurt

6 garlic cloves, chopped

½ bunch fresh mint, hand-torn

½ bunch fresh cilantro, hand-torn

Extra-virgin olive oil

Sea salt and freshly ground black pepper

Start by roasting the peppers for the harissa. Preheat the broiler. Pull out the cores of the red peppers; then halve them lengthwise and remove the ribs and seeds. Place them on a cookie sheet, skin side up, and broil for 10 minutes, until really charred and blistered. Put the peppers into a bowl, cover with plastic wrap, and steam for about 10 minutes to loosen the skins; then peel. Toast the cumin, coriander, and caraway seeds in a dry skillet over low heat until fragrant, shaking the pan so they don't scorch. In a clean coffee grinder or spice mill, grind the spices to a powder and then put them in a food processor with the roasted peppers, garlic, chiles, salt, and oil. Pulse until the sauce is well blended and smooth, adding a little more oil to thin it out, if necessary. Set the harissa aside while preparing the caponata.

Pour the oil into a large, deep skillet set over medium heat. Add the anchovies and red pepper flakes. Cook and stir for a few minutes to create a base flavor. Fry the eggplant until it absorbs the oil and browns, stirring often. Add the tomatoes, onion, and garlic, and continue to cook until the vegetables break down and soften, about 15 minutes. Toss in the capers, raisins, pine nuts, balsamic vinegar, sugar, and basil; season with salt and pepper. Lower the heat and slowly simmer until thick, about 20 minutes. Add the figs in the last 5 minutes of cooking to soften them slightly. The caponata tastes superb hot, cold, or at room temperature.

Preheat a gas or charcoal grill and get it very hot. Lay the lamb out on a flat surface and open it like a book. Mix together the yogurt, garlic, mint, and cilantro and spread an even, thin layer over the meat. Roll it up and tie it with butcher's twine like you would a roast. If you have time, let the lamb sit for 1 hour. Drizzle the roast with oil and season generously with salt and pepper. Cut the roast in half crosswise so it's easier to handle and cooks quicker. Take a few paper towels and fold them several times to make a thick square. Blot a small amount of oil on the paper towel; then carefully and quickly wipe the hot grates of the grill. Put the lamb roasts on the outer part of the grill so the outside doesn't burn before the inside is cooked. Grill until the meat is nicely browned on all sides, about 1 hour. The lamb is medium-rare when the internal temperature reads 130°F.; it will still be pink inside. Allow the roasts to stand for 10 minutes to let the juices settle before cutting off the twine and slicing.

Oven Variation

Preheat the oven to 350°F. Set the lamb roasts fat side up in a roasting pan and put them in the oven. After 1 hour, start testing for doneness. Proceed as above.

Note: In the great Middle Eastern restaurants in my neighborhood, they serve something similar to this wrapped in naan, an Indian bread. Fill a naan bread or pita with a large spoon of the caponata and a few slices of lamb and a little of the harissa, then roll it together. Green onions, mint, and yogurt make great garnishes.

New York Strip Steaks with Grilled Fennel Salad and Paprika Butter

 **1 hour**

Infused butters are fun to put together because you can customize different flavors to give grilled meats a whole new dimension. This dish has strong roots in the Spanish Mediterranean countryside, and it's one of the hits of this chapter.

Serves 4

Paprika Butter

4 roasted garlic cloves
3 anchovy fillets
1½ tablespoons sweet paprika
½ cup (1 stick) unsalted butter, softened

Grilled Fennel Salad

4 small fennel bulbs, tops removed, sliced into
  ½-inch rings
4 black plums, halved and pitted
Extra-virgin olive oil
Sea salt and freshly ground black pepper
½ cup pitted green Spanish olives
¼ bunch fresh basil
Pinch of red pepper flakes
1 teaspoon ground coriander
Juice of ½ lemon

Steaks

4 New York strip steaks, 10 ounces each
Extra-virgin olive oil
Sea salt and freshly ground black pepper

In a food processor, combine the roasted garlic with the anchovies and pulse them a couple of times to make a paste. Add the paprika and butter; puree until the ingredients are well blended and the butter is red. Set it aside at room temperature.

Put the fennel rings and plums on a sheet pan and drizzle with a 3-count of oil; season with salt and pepper. In a separate bowl, put the remaining salad ingredients: the olives, basil, red pepper flakes, coriander, and lemon juice. Drizzle with a 2-count of oil, season with salt and pepper, and give the salad a good toss. Let the olive mixture sit out and marinate while you do the grilling.

Preheat a gas or charcoal grill and get it very hot. Rub both sides of the steaks with oil; season them with a generous amount of salt and pepper. Take a few paper towels and fold them several times to make a thick square. Blot a small amount of oil on the paper towel; then carefully and quickly wipe the hot grates of the grill. This will create a nonstick grilling surface. Grill the steaks for about 7 minutes per side for medium-rare. While the steaks are working, put the fennel on the free side of the grill and grill for 5 minutes per side. In the last 5 minutes of cooking, put the plums on the grill, cut side down, so the flesh softens and caramelizes slightly but doesn't get mushy. Take everything off the grill and let the steak rest while you put the salad together.

Cut the plums into quarters and add them to the olive mixture; add the fennel rings and toss the entire salad together. This salad is best when the fennel and plums are still warm, so lather the steak with the paprika butter and serve it with the salad ASAP.

Cold Fried Chicken

 1 hour + marinating and chilling time

Really, is there anything better than opening up your fridge to find some beautiful cold fried chicken looking back at you? You glance to the left, you glance to the right. Nobody in sight. You don't even bother with a plate, maybe just a paper towel. Maybe nothing at all. And then it's yours, all yours to nibble at until you're done and licking your fingers. Oh, yeah, this chicken's also great for picnics (if there is any left over). Maintaining even oil temperature is key. That way the crust doesn't balloon away from the skin but becomes part of it. You'll need an electric fryer with a built-in thermometer, or use a clip-on deep-fry thermometer and a deep-sided skillet.

Serves 4

1 frying chicken, 3½ pounds, cut into 8 serving pieces
2 cups buttermilk
¼ cup water
2 teaspoons Tabasco sauce
3 cups all-purpose flour
1 tablespoon garlic powder
1 tablespoon onion powder
2 teaspoons sweet paprika
2 teaspoons cayenne
Sea salt and freshly ground black pepper
Canola oil, for frying

Rinse the chicken pieces and pat dry with paper towels. In a large bowl, combine the buttermilk, water, and Tabasco. Soak the chicken pieces, turning to coat, then cover and refrigerate for at least 2 hours. If time allows, marinate the chicken for up to 24 hours so that the buttermilk will have a chance to tenderize the chicken.

Place the flour in a large shallow platter. Add the garlic powder, onion powder, paprika, and cayenne; season with lots of salt and pepper. Mix the seasoned flour together with your fingers so that all the ingredients are thoroughly incorporated. Taste the flour; it should have a nice balance of seasoning. Roll the marinated chicken pieces in the flour, a few at a time, until well coated. Bathe the chicken in the buttermilk again and then roll it around in the seasoned flour one more time. Let the chicken sit in the flour and dry out while you heat the oil; this will help the crust stay on better. The buttermilk will be absorbed by the seasoned flour, which then fries up to form a crunchy crust.

Heat 1 inch of oil in a large skillet or electric fryer to 375°F. I like the oil very hot to start out with because as soon as the chicken is added, the temperature drops significantly. Working in batches, carefully add 3 or 4 pieces of chicken in a single layer, skin side down. Fry for 5 minutes; then turn the pieces over and fry the other side for 5 minutes. Make sure the fat continues to bubble around the chicken; lift the chicken pieces with tongs now and again to check for even browning. Continue to turn and fry a total of 20 minutes until you've got a golden, crisp skin with even color. Remove the chicken to a platter lined with paper towels and repeat with the remaining pieces. Let the chicken cool to room temperature before storing. Fried chicken that's covered while it's hot has a tendency to steam and the crust may sog. Refrigerate for several hours before serving.

Spiced Calamari Skewers with Grilled Lime

 **1 hour**

Grilled calamari is a big hit at cocktail parties. It sounds exotic and the platter always comes back empty. The spice mix gives this particular recipe a serious Caribbean influence, and right before the skewers go out I squeeze the grilled lime over the top. Have your fishmonger clean the squid for you. You will need wooden skewers, and don't forget to soak them in water for 20 minutes before you use them.

Makes 40 pieces

1 tablespoon curry powder

1 teaspoon cumin seed

1 teaspoon fennel seed

1 teaspoon whole black peppercorns

1 teaspoon cayenne

1 tablespoon sea salt

20 small whole calamari, cleaned, tentacles
  reserved for another use

Extra-virgin olive oil

4 limes, halved

Put the curry, cumin, fennel, peppercorns, cayenne, and salt in a spice mill or clean coffee grinder. Grind to a fine powder and set aside.

Rinse the calamari tubes under cool water and pat dry. Split the bodies from top to bottom so you have 2 triangular pieces from each. Thread a skewer through the length of each piece to secure. Put the skewered calamari on a platter and drizzle with a 3-count of oil. Place a large grill pan on 2 burners over medium-high heat, or preheat a gas or charcoal grill. Fold a few paper towels into a thick square. Blot some oil on the paper towels and then carefully and quickly wipe the ridges of the grill pan or the hot grates of the grill. Grill the calamari for 2 minutes per side (no longer or they will get rubbery). Place the limes on the grill, cut side down, for 2 minutes or until slightly charred.

Sprinkle a little of the spice mix on the calamari and stack the skewers on a serving platter. Squeeze the grilled limes over the calamari and serve immediately.

Roasted Vegetable Muffuletta with Black Olive Tapenade

 **1 hour**

This is a fat, stuffed vegetable sandwich that's great for a picnic. The olive tapenade is also good spooned on bread toasts and served as an hors d'oeuvre.

Serves 6 to 8 ★ **Makes 1½ cups tapenade**

Muffuletta

1 red bell pepper, halved, stem and seeds
  removed

1 yellow bell pepper, halved, stem and seeds
  removed

1 zucchini, sliced in ¼-inch circles

1 yellow squash, sliced in ¼-inch circles

1 small eggplant, sliced in ¼-inch circles

1 red onion, sliced in ¼-inch circles

1 tomato, sliced in ¼-inch circles

3 large portobello mushrooms, stems removed,
  cut into ¼-inch thick slices

4 garlic cloves, unpeeled

¾ cup extra-virgin olive oil

Juice of 1 lemon

Sea salt and freshly ground black pepper

1 large round Tuscan bread or French boule

1 pound mozzarella cheese, sliced ¼ inch thick

Black Olive Tapenade

½ pound kalamata olives, pitted

3 anchovy fillets

2 tablespoons capers, drained

1 tablespoon red wine vinegar

¼ teaspoon red pepper flakes

5 basil leaves, hand-torn

¼ cup extra-virgin olive oil

Preheat the oven to 450°F. Put the vegetables in a large bowl and toss them with the oil, lemon juice, and salt and pepper, turning to coat. Lay the vegetables in a single layer on cookie sheets (the peppers should be skin side up) and bake for 30 minutes, until well roasted. Put the peppers into a bowl, cover with plastic wrap, and let steam for about 10 minutes to loosen the skins; then peel. Reserve the roasted garlic cloves for the olive tapenade. Set the rest of the vegetables aside to cool to room temperature.

Peel the skins off the roasted garlic. In a food processor, combine the olives, anchovies, capers, red wine vinegar, red pepper flakes, basil, oil, and roasted garlic cloves. Pulse until the mixture is well blended.

To make the sandwich, cut the bread loaf in half horizontally. Pull out all but 1 inch of the bread from the inside of each half to create a cavity. Spread the tapenade in one even layer inside the bread, making sure to do both halves. You will have a little olive paste left over; set it aside for the vegetables. Start stacking the roasted vegetables inside the bottom half of the bread. I like to keep the colors together; it looks nicer when you cut it that way. Season each layer with salt and pepper. Alternate every third layer with mozzarella and then a little of the olive tapenade. Stack the vegetables in a slight pyramid formation so the top will fit. Continue layering the vegetables and cheese until the loaf is full and all the vegetables have been used. Cap the sandwich with the top half of the bread and press it slightly. Place the muffuletta on the center of a very big piece of plastic wrap. Fold the plastic over the top to cover and then twist the ends really tight to compress the sandwich. When ready to eat, slice the sandwich like a pie with a serrated knife.

Clambake

 **2 hours**

Beach clambakes are a blast. They make me think of Annette Funicello, who I still find very attractive. Anyway . . . Lobsters, clams, and corn all steamed in seaweed: For me, it's the perfect summer party. Even if you can't get to the beach, you can still pull off a great clambake in your own backyard. Be sure to ask your fish guy for some seaweed. Lobsters come in crates packed with this stuff, so he should be able to give you some. Parboil the lobsters to kill them first before putting them on the grill. Alternatively, you can just split the bodies down the middle to kill them and skip the boiling step.

Serves 4 to 8

4 lobsters

5 pounds seaweed

12 new potatoes

4 ears corn

2 kielbasa sausages, halved lengthwise

2 dozen littleneck clams

2 dozen oysters

Lemon wedges, for garnish

Melted butter, for dipping

Preheat your grill until it's fairly hot. Meanwhile, bring a large pot of salted water to a boil. Parboil the lobsters for just 3 minutes and then remove. To start the outdoor clambake, spread a thick layer of seaweed directly on the hot grill rack. The potatoes and corn go down first since they will take the longest to cook. Arrange the potatoes and corn on the seaweed in a single layer, then cover them with more seaweed. Put the lobsters on top, along with the kielbasa; cover with more seaweed. Spread the clams on top and cover with another layer of seaweed. Finally, set the oysters on the top, and blanket them with a thick layer of seaweed. As the seafood cooks, the juices will drip down and flavor the corn and potatoes. Cover the entire bake with a burlap bag that has been soaked in water; it traps in the seaweed steam and bakes the food. Cover the grill. Cook until the clams open and the lobsters are bright red, about 1 to 1½ hours. Keep a bucket of water handy and check the burlap periodically to make sure it stays wet. Serve with lemon wedges and melted butter.

Grilled Salmon with Watermelon and Black Olive Salad

 **1 hour**

The black olive and watermelon are a perfect salty-sweet yin-yang that goes great with the grilled salmon. This is a very crisp, refreshing dish for a summer cookout—like a cool drink of water. This vinaigrette is good on almost anything, so save any that is left over and use it within the week.

Serves 4 ★ Makes 1 cup vinaigrette

Salad

4 cups cubed seedless watermelon

½ cup kalamata olives, pitted

½ red onion, sliced thin

1 large bunch arugula, trimmed

Vinaigrette

½ teaspoon ground cardamom

½ teaspoon ground cinnamon

½ teaspoon cumin seed

½ teaspoon fennel seed

1 teaspoon sugar

¼ cup sherry vinegar

¾ cup extra-virgin olive oil

Sea salt and freshly ground black pepper

Salmon

4 salmon fillets, 6 to 8 ounces each, skin on, about 1 inch thick

Extra-virgin olive oil

Sea salt and freshly ground black pepper

To make the salad, toss the watermelon, black olives, red onion, and arugula together in a bowl. Put it in the fridge to chill. The contrast of a cold salad with the hot salmon is really refreshing.

To make the vinaigrette, toast the spices in a dry skillet over low heat for 1 minute, until they smell fragrant; shake the pan frequently to prevent scorching. In a spice mill or clean coffee grinder, grind the toasted spices with the sugar. Put the sherry vinegar and oil in a blender and add the ground spice mixture; give it all a whirl to blend. Season with salt and pepper.

Preheat a gas or charcoal grill and get it very hot. Rub both sides of the salmon with oil; then season with a generous amount of salt and pepper. Take a few paper towels and fold them several times to make a thick square. Blot a small amount of oil on the paper towel. Then carefully and quickly wipe the hot grates of the grill. This will create a nonstick grilling surface. Grill the salmon, skin side down, for 5 minutes. Carefully turn the fillets over and grill the other side for another 5 minutes, until the fish is opaque.

Toss half the vinaigrette with the salad; wait until right before serving to prevent the arugula from wilting. Serve the grilled salmon on top of the salad family style. Easy McEasy.

Grilled Scallops with Grilled Endive, Cantaloupe, and Mint

 **45 minutes**

Opposites definitely attract: The slightly bitter endive married with the sweet cantaloupe. It's a perfect summer dish and incredibly easy . . . what more do you want?

Serves 4 to 6

24 sea scallops, about 2 pounds
6 heads Belgian endive
Extra-virgin olive oil
Sea salt and freshly ground black pepper
1 cantaloupe, peeled and cut into small chunks
½ bunch fresh mint
1 small fresh red chile, cut into paper-thin circles
2 green onions, cut into paper-thin circles
Pinch of sugar
Juice of 1 lemon

Start by assessing the scallops at the fish store. I usually inspect every one just to make sure that they're all in perfect shape—not torn, and fresh with a sweet ocean smell. If you're not convinced the scallops are at their peak, use shrimp instead. Lay the scallops on a paper towel to drain any excess natural liquid; wet scallops do not cook well. Soak 16 wooden skewers in water for 20 minutes or so. Next remove the side muscle that connects the scallop to its shell. It's not hard to miss; just pull it off with your fingers. Line up 3 scallops in a row and thread 2 skewers through the sides, going all the way through. Using 2 skewers gives the delicate scallops support and makes them much easier to turn. Use sharp kitchen shears to trim off the excess wood from the sticks. Put the scallop skewers on a large platter.

Preheat a gas or charcoal grill and get it very hot. Take a few paper towels and fold them several times to make a thick square. Blot a small amount of oil on the paper towel and then carefully and quickly wipe the hot grates of the grill. This will create a nonstick grilling surface.

Cut the heads of endive in half lengthwise. Brush with a little oil; season with salt and pepper. Put the endive halves, cut side down, on the grill. When they start to brown and caramelize slightly, turn them over with tongs. Take them off the grill when they are somewhat softened but still holding together. The endive should take 5 minutes per side. Let the endive cool a bit, and move on to the scallops. They take a few minutes to grill up.

Brush the scallops with oil; season with salt and pepper. Put them on the hot grill for 3 to 4 minutes per side until they have a nice char. Scallops are a little delicate—if one seems to stick don't try to pull it up, you will tear the damn thing. Give it 30 seconds and then try again. Remove the scallops from the skewers.

To put it all together, split the cooled endive halves lengthwise into wedges and put them in a bowl with the cantaloupe, mint, chile, green onions, and sugar. Squeeze the lemon juice over and then drizzle with a 3-count of olive oil; season with salt and pepper. Toss gently to mix everything together. Add the scallops and carefully toss with the cantaloupe and endive, finishing with several turns of freshly ground black pepper. Serve 4 to 6 scallops per person with a cold glass of sauvignon blanc.

"I get a buzz from having people over, and whether it's a casual dinner party or a sunset cookout, the food is simple, and everyone has a good time."

the cocktail party

I have to admit that a few times a year I like to throw a blowout party—the kind of party that is so packed with people that you really don't know everyone there. For such occasions, it's important to take a few days to plan what you're going to make and serve. Being organized is very important when preparing serious hors d'oeuvres. I'm not talking about a cheese plate and cocktail weenies, I'm talking about beautiful, original hors d'oeuvres. This section will give you ideas, crystal-clear instructions, and recipes so amazing that your guests will be convinced that a restaurant catered your party, plus directions for twelve cocktails that will let you flex your mixology muscles and get the evening hopping.

Prosciutto-Roasted Figs

 **45 minutes**

These little gems are what I like to think of as new-wave pigs in a blanket. The ham and fruit are a perfect balance of salty and sweet, and a sip of champagne complements the flavors perfectly.

Makes 40 pieces

40 small fresh Mission figs
4 ounces manchego cheese or blue cheese
20 slices prosciutto, halved lengthwise
⅓ cup honey
Freshly ground black pepper

Preheat the oven to 400°F. Make a small slit in the side of each fig and stuff a raisin-size piece of cheese in the opening. Wrap a piece of prosciutto around each fig to enclose it in a little cocoon. Stand the figs on a sheet pan. Bake for 12 to 15 minutes so the prosciutto melts slightly and forms a skin around the figs. Drizzle with honey and season with lots of ground black pepper. These are terrific hot or at room temp.

Grape and Blue Cheese Truffles

 **20 minutes**

Everyone will be blown away by how simple these are. They will be the runaway hit of the night. The moisture and sweetness of the grape inside the cheese is a flavor burst.

Serves 20

4 ounces cream cheese, softened

8 ounces blue cheese, softened

3 tablespoons port

1 bunch seedless white grapes, about 2 pounds

1 cup pistachios, ground

Mash the cream cheese and blue cheese together in a bowl until combined. Pour in the port and mix until blended. Grab a bit of the cheese in one hand and a grape in the other. Put the two together and roll the grape around in your hands until it is completely covered by the cheese. Roll the cheese-covered grapes in the ground pistachios. Chill until ready to serve.

Vietnamese Shrimp Rolls with Sweet Chili Dipping Sauce

 1½ hours   Photo on page 203

These spring rolls are so fresh tasting that they're addictive. The beet turns the noodles a pretty pink—way cool. Wear gloves when you cut up the beet so your hands don't turn purple—not a festive look.

Makes 20 rolls ＊ Makes 1⅓ cups sauce

3 ounces Vietnamese cellophane noodles, cooked according to package directions

2 cups bean sprouts

2 carrots, thinly sliced

1 large beet, thinly sliced

1 fresh red chile, cut into circles

¼ cup chopped fresh cilantro

¾ cup chopped salted peanuts

2 teaspoons sesame oil

Juice of 1 lime

Sea salt and freshly ground black pepper

1 teaspoon sugar

20 (8-inch) round rice paper wrappers

20 cooked medium shrimp, tails off, halved lengthwise

40 mint leaves

Sweet Chili Dipping Sauce

¼ cup rice wine vinegar

2 tablespoons fish sauce

¼ cup hot water

2 tablespoons sugar

Juice of 1 lime

1 teaspoon minced garlic

1 teaspoon red chili paste, such as sambal

2 tablespoons grated carrot

2 tablespoons grated daikon radish

>>

Put the cellophane noodles, vegetables, cilantro, and peanuts in a bowl; toss with the sesame oil and lime juice to give the filling some flavor; season with salt and pepper. In a large shallow bowl, dilute the sugar in 3 cups of hot water and give it a stir. One at a time, immerse the rice paper spring roll wrappers in the hot water for 10 seconds and then place on a damp towel. The rice paper is very delicate; don't soak them any longer or they will break apart. Keep them covered while you work to prevent them from drying out and curling. To form the rolls, lay a rice paper wrapper on a flat surface. Grab a small amount of the cellophane noodle and vegetable mixture and lay it across the bottom third. Use less filling than you think you should; if you overstuff the wrapper it will tear. Carefully fold the bottom of the wrapper up to cover the filling. Fold in the left and right sides, then tuck and roll it over once. Lay 2 pieces of shrimp on top, then tuck and roll it over again. Lay 2 mint leaves on top and then tuck and roll it over to close the whole thing up like a tight cigar. The shrimp and mint leaves should show through the transparent rice paper. Arrange the finished rolls on a platter and cover with a damp towel.

In a blender, puree the rice wine vinegar, fish sauce, hot water, sugar, lime juice, garlic, and chili paste until combined. Pour into a serving bowl. Add the grated carrot and radish and mix. Serve the shrimp rolls with the sweet chili dipping sauce. These also make a terrific light lunch.

Marinated Raw Tuna with Edamame Puree and Wonton Crisps

 1½ hours including marinating time

The wonton crisps can be made a day before and stored in an airtight container. They are good for snacking, so don't eat them all. Edamame are green soybeans in their pods. The edamame puree will blow people; it has a creamy consistency with a hot wasabi punch, and it's also a terrific dip. I find pinching the soybeans out of their pods somewhat therapeutic, kind of like popping bubble wrap.

Makes 40 pieces ✳ Makes 1½ cups puree

Wonton Crisps

½ cup sesame oil

40 wonton skins

Edamame Puree

1-pound package frozen soybeans in their pods

1 tablespoon wasabi powder or paste

1 teaspoon sea salt

Juice of 1 lemon

6 tablespoons water

2 tablespoons canola oil

Marinated Tuna

½ cup low-sodium soy sauce

2 tablespoons sake

2 tablespoons brown sugar

1 teaspoon red chili paste, such as sambal

1 pound sushi-quality tuna, such as ahi (yellowfin) or bluefin, cut into ¼-inch strips

2 tablespoons sesame seeds, toasted, for garnish (see Note, page 34)

more like 8!

Preheat the oven to 350°F. Brush a couple of cookie sheets with sesame oil. Lay the wonton skins side by side in a single layer. Brush the surface of the wontons with the oil. Bake for 15 minutes, until the wontons crisp up and the edges are golden. Using a spatula, remove the wonton crisps to a platter to let them cool.

Blanch the soybeans in boiling salted water for 5 minutes. Drain, pinch the beans out of their pods, and put them in a food processor. Add the wasabi, salt, lemon juice, and water. Puree to break up the soybeans. Pour in the canola oil and puree until smooth. Refrigerate.

Whisk together the soy sauce, sake, brown sugar, and chili paste until the sugar dissolves. Arrange the sliced tuna in a single layer in a shallow dish. Pour the marinade over the tuna, cover, and refrigerate for 20 minutes. Don't marinate the tuna any longer because it will start to "cook" and the texture will be mushy.

To put these little gems together, dollop a spoonful of the edamame puree on the wonton crisp and then lay a slice of tuna on the top. Garnish with a sprinkle of toasted sesame seeds. Outstanding. Always the hit of the party.

Dates Wrapped in Bacon with Green Olive Sauce

 **1 hour**

This very Spanish-influenced tapa hits your tongue in three-stage flavor assault. First the smoky bacon, next the slightly salty green olive sauce, then the sweetness of the date. But the kicker is the almond inside—the little crunch that totally takes you by surprise. The combo is unique and classic, and I like to up the presentation with fancy toothpicks.

Makes 40 pieces * Makes 1⅔ cups sauce

Dates

40 whole almonds, with skin
40 dates, about 1½ pounds, pitted
20 bacon slices, halved

Green Olive Sauce

Extra-virgin olive oil
2 shallots, sliced
1 dried red chile, minced
½ pound green Spanish olives, pitted
¼ bunch fresh flat-leaf parsley
2 tablespoons sherry vinegar

Preheat the oven to 350°F. Lay the almonds on a cookie sheet in a single layer. Bake for 10 minutes or until the nuts are lightly toasted. Remove from the oven. When cool enough to handle, stuff an almond inside each date. Wrap a piece of bacon around the date so the ends stick together. Put them on cookie sheets and bake until the bacon is crisp, 20 to 25 minutes. While that is happening, make the olive sauce.

In a small skillet, heat a 2-count drizzle of oil. Sauté the shallots and chile over low heat for 8 minutes, until caramelized. Let them cool a bit and then scrape them into a food processor. Add the olives, parsley, vinegar, and ½ cup of oil. Puree a good 3 minutes, until totally smooth. Serve the dates with the olive sauce for dipping and some funky toothpicks. *Delicioso!*

Cured Sardine Toasts
with Red Pepper and Basil

 1½ hours including curing time   Photo on page 194

This hors d'oeuvre is straight from the tapas bars of southern Spain. A few of these with a glass of sangría and I'm in heaven. It's important to have your local fish guy fillet the sardines for you and save yourself the hassle. Spanish paprika is truly an underrated spice—it has a very satisfying smoky flavor that intensifies the taste of the roasted peppers. I have been experimenting with it in everything lately because I love its depth.

Makes 24 pieces

2 pounds small whole sardines, filleted, about 24 pieces

1 orange, unpeeled and thinly sliced

½ cup sherry vinegar

2 tablespoons white sherry

4 garlic cloves, minced

2 bay leaves, crumbled

1 teaspoon sugar

1 teaspoon sea salt

Extra-virgin olive oil

5 red bell peppers

1½ teaspoons sweet paprika, preferably Spanish

Sea salt and freshly ground black pepper

1 baguette, sliced into 24 (1-inch) circles

1 bunch fresh basil

½ cup pine nuts, toasted and ground

Arrange the sardines in a single layer, flesh side down, in a shallow dish. Lay the orange slices on top of the sardines. Mix together the sherry vinegar, sherry, garlic, bay leaves, sugar, salt, and a 4-count of oil. Pour the marinade over the sardines and oranges; cover and let cure in the refrigerator for 30 minutes.

Preheat the broiler. Pull out the tops of the red peppers; then cut them in half lengthwise and remove the seeds. Place the peppers on a cookie sheet, skin side up, and broil for about 10 minutes to let them really char and blister. Put the peppers into a bowl, cover with plastic wrap, and steam for about 10 minutes to loosen the skins; then peel. Slice the peppers into 3-inch pieces and toss with the paprika and a 4-count of oil. Season the pepper strips with salt and pepper.

Preheat the oven to 350°F. Brush each side of the bread slices with oil and place on a cookie sheet. Bake for 10 minutes, until toasty and golden.

To put these beauties together, lay a piece of roasted pepper on each toasted bread slice. Stick a large basil leaf on top. Remove the sardine slices from the orange marinade and slice them in half so they will fit nicely on the toasted bread. Lay the sardines, skin side up, across the basil. Finish it up with a sprinkle of toasted pine nuts and serve. This truly is the perfect bite!

Slow-Roasted Spanish Olives with Oranges and Almonds

 2 hours 10 minutes

These are my girlfriend's favorite. I make them in batches to have in the fridge to snack on.

Serves 20

2 pounds Spanish olives, such as manzanilla or gordal, with pits
1 orange, unpeeled, sliced into ⅛-inch circles
1 cup whole almonds, with skin
¼ cup sherry vinegar
1 cup extra-virgin olive oil
2 bay leaves
10 fresh thyme sprigs
1 red chile pepper, halved lengthwise

Preheat the oven to 300°F. Combine the olives and the remaining ingredients in a mixing bowl. Transfer the mixture to a baking dish, cover with foil, and bake for 2 hours. Drain the oil out (keep it to use as a bread dip) and serve the olives warm or at room temperature with assorted cheeses.

Steak Tartare with Parmigiano Frico

 **1 hour**

I order steak tartare in restaurants whenever it's on the menu. When you serve it at home it's important to seek a fine butcher who can provide you with the best-quality beef. You can make the Parmigiano baskets the morning of the party and store them covered at room temperature; they will still have an amazing snap hours later. The trick for success with this is not to use "green can" grated cheese, which will not melt evenly; you have to buy the good stuff. Once you get the hang of making Parmigiano-Reggiano frico you can really crank them out. The tops of water or soda bottles are ideal for forming the Parmigiano cups. I also like to make flat frico as a crunchy garnish for Caesar salads.

Makes 40 pieces

2 cups coarsely grated Parmigiano-Reggiano cheese

1¼ pounds lean sirloin, trimmed of excess fat

Sea salt and freshly ground black pepper

2 egg yolks (see Note)

1 anchovy fillet, chopped

2 teaspoons Dijon mustard

1 teaspoon red chili paste, such as sambal

1 teaspoon Worcestershire sauce

Juice of ½ lemon

½ red onion, finely diced

1 tablespoon capers, drained and minced

¼ cup chopped fresh flat-leaf parsley

1 tablespoon extra-virgin olive oil

2 tablespoons chopped fresh chives, for garnish

Heat a small, nonstick skillet over medium-low heat. Sprinkle 1 tablespoon of the Parmigiano in the center of the pan, making a circle about 3 inches in diameter. Cook until the cheese melts and the cheese strands intertwine like a web, about 2 minutes. Don't touch the cheese until the bottom starts to get lightly golden. Then press the cheese down with the bottom of a spatula so it sets. Take the pan off the heat for a second to let the cheese round set. Carefully remove the cheese round from the pan and place it over the top of a water or soda bottle. While it is still hot, press the cheese down so it forms a cup shape; let it cool and harden. This will be the edible container for the tartare.

Right before you plan to serve this, cut the beef into cubes and put it in the food processor. Pulse the steak until it looks like ground beef. Transfer the meat to a bowl and fold in all the remaining ingredients except the chives. Season with salt and pepper.

Put a teaspoonful of the steak tartare into each Parmigiano cup. Garnish with chopped chives and serve immediately. I recommend filling the cheese cups in batches so the meat doesn't sog the bottom.

Note: *Healthy people need to remember that there is a very small risk associated with eating raw eggs. Use only properly refrigerated, clean, sound-shelled, fresh, grade AA or A eggs. Avoid mixing yolks and whites with the shell.*

Chilled Pea Shots
with Spicy Crab

 30 minutes + chilling time

The thing about hors d'oeuvres is that they should not only taste good, but they should look really cool, too. These do just that. You need espresso cups, sake cups, or fancy shot glasses for these. These "pea shooters" are great to make ahead and put together at the last minute. Drinking an hors d'oeuvre is the cool way to go!

Serves 15

Pea Soup

2 cups frozen sweet peas, run under cool water
   to thaw
1 (14½-ounce) can vegetable broth
½ cup canola oil
½ teaspoon freshly squeezed lemon juice
Sea salt and freshly ground black pepper

Spicy Crab

3 tablespoons canola oil
1 tablespoon red chili paste, such as sambal
Juice of ½ lemon
1 cup fresh lump crabmeat, picked through
¼ bunch fresh mint, chopped
Pinch of sea salt

Blend the peas and vegetable broth in a blender until smooth. Take the lid off and, with the motor running, pour in the oil in a steady stream until the mixture is emulsified. Add the lemon juice, season with salt and pepper, and then chill in the refrigerator for 1 hour.

To make the spicy crab, whisk the canola oil, chili paste, and lemon juice together in a bowl. Fold in the crabmeat and mint and season with a pinch of salt. Fill espresso or sake cups about three-quarters full with the chilled pea soup. Garnish the pea shots with a generous tablespoon of the spicy crab and serve right away.

Teriyaki Chicken Wings with Sesame and Cilantro

 **1 hour**

Chicken wings don't have to be just chicken wings. This teriyaki glaze is incredibly easy to make and turns a boring concept into something sophisticated.

Serves 6 ★ Makes 2½ cups sauce

Teriyaki Sauce

1 cup low-sodium soy sauce

1 cup grapefruit juice

¼ cup hoisin sauce

¼ cup ketchup

3 tablespoons rice wine vinegar

¼ cup brown sugar

1 fresh red chile, halved

5 garlic cloves, halved

2-inch piece fresh ginger, smashed

Chicken Wings

2 dozen chicken wings, about 3¼ pounds, rinsed and patted dry

Sea salt and freshly ground black pepper

1 tablespoon sesame seeds, toasted, for garnish (see Note, page 34)

½ bunch fresh cilantro, chopped, for garnish

Prepare the teriyaki sauce by combining the soy sauce, grapefruit juice, hoisin sauce, ketchup, rice wine vinegar, brown sugar, chile, garlic, and ginger in a pot. Bring to a slow boil and cook, stirring, until thickened, about 20 minutes.

Preheat the oven to 400°F. Season the chicken wings generously with salt and pepper. Lay the chicken wings in a single layer on a sheet pan. Bake for 20 minutes or until the skin gets crispy. With tongs, dip the wings in the teriyaki sauce and return them to the oven for 10 minutes to glaze. An impressive presentation is to serve these chicken wings family style: Arrange them on a large platter, pour over the remaining sauce, and sprinkle them with the sesame seeds and cilantro. Serve the wings with a large stack of cocktail napkins.

Curried Deviled Eggs with Salmon Caviar

 **1 hour**

People love these, and the salmon caviar gives this classic an updated twist.

Makes 24

1 dozen eggs
6 tablespoons mayonnaise
1 tablespoon Dijon mustard
Juice of 1 lemon
1 tablespoon curry powder
1 teaspoon cayenne
Sea salt and freshly ground black pepper
1 ounce salmon caviar, for garnish
¼ bunch fresh chives, minced, for garnish

Put the eggs in your largest pot and cover with 1 inch of water. Bring to a boil over high heat. Once the water boils, turn off the heat, cover the pot, and let the eggs sit in the hot water for 20 minutes. Cool the eggs by running them under cool water. Peel them and cut them in half lengthwise. Carefully scoop the egg yolks into a food processor. Add the mayonnaise, Dijon mustard, lemon juice, curry, cayenne, and salt and pepper and puree until smooth.

Classically, the yolk filling is piped into the egg white using a pastry bag fitted with a star tip. This presentation is very old school but it's actually a really quick method, too. If you prefer, use a teaspoon to fill the eggs. They'll look great either way. Garnish the eggs with the caviar and chives.

Salmon Gravlax

 1 day to cure the salmon ★ 2 hours for everything else

This takes a little planning but the effort is well worth it. The salmon gravlax takes 5 minutes to put together and about 24 hours to cure in the salt. The flavor is fresh and buttery. Super-fresh fish is a must.

Serves 20

Salmon Gravlax

1 lemon

1 cup coarse sea salt

½ cup sugar

½ bunch fresh dill

2-pound side of salmon, 1 inch thick,
   pin bones removed, skin on

Buckwheat Blini

1 package active dry yeast

1½ cups warm milk

1 cup all-purpose flour

½ cup buckwheat flour

½ teaspoon salt

1 teaspoon sugar

4 tablespoons unsalted butter, melted, plus more for sautéing

3 eggs, separated

Dill Crème Fraîche

½ cup crème fraîche

½ bunch fresh dill, coarsely chopped

Juice of ½ lemon

1 teaspoon sea salt

Remove the zest of the lemon with a vegetable peeler in fat strips and toss it in a bowl. Add the salt, sugar, and dill; toss to combine. Lay the fish in a large glass baking dish. Pack the salt mixture on and around the salmon. Cover and refrigerate for 24 hours to cure the fish.

To make the blini, dissolve the yeast in the warm milk and then let it proof for 10 minutes. Sift the all-purpose flour, buckwheat flour, salt, and sugar together in a bowl. Pour the yeast mixture into a blender along with the dry ingredients. Puree on high until smooth. Scrape down the sides of the blender, add the melted butter and egg yolks (reserve the whites), and process again until combined. Pour the batter into a large bowl, cover with a towel, and let it rise in a warm place for 1½ hours.

Just before you are ready to cook the blini, beat the egg whites until stiff; then fold them into the batter. Place a griddle or nonstick skillet over medium-high heat and brush with a little melted butter. Pour 1 tablespoon at a time of batter into the pan to make pancakes about 3 inches in diameter. Cook for about 30 seconds, then flip them over with a spatula and cook for another 30 seconds. Stack the blini on a platter and wrap them in a cloth napkin to keep them warm.

Combine the ingredients for the crème fraîche.

Scrape the salt mixture off the salmon and lightly rinse the fish under cool water. Pat dry with paper towels. The cured salmon will be firm but pliable. To set up the presentation, lay the salmon on a large wooden cutting board. With a very sharp knife slice the salmon New York Deli–style: paper-thin and on a slight angle. (The whole fish looks great as a centerpiece on the table, so slice only a quarter of the salmon at a time.) Serve the salmon with the blini and condiments on the side. This is an interactive hors d'oeuvre: Let your friends attack it and then slice more as needed. Always a huge hit.

Oyster Shucking

Scrub the oysters under cold water to remove the dirt, especially from the hinge area, where mud has a tendency to get trapped. Next, find a durable thick cloth and fold it over several times to create a square. This will steady the oysters as you shuck them and also will protect your hand.

Using the towel as a mitt, place the oyster, cup side down, in the palm of your hand with the hinge facing you. Insert the tip of an oyster knife or dull butter knife as far into the hinge as it will go; don't jab it in there or you could break the shell. With gentle force, twist the knife back and forth to pry the shell open. Using the knife, cut the muscle away from the top shell, bend the shell back, and discard it. Run the knife underneath the oyster to detach it completely, but leave it in the shell. Be careful not to spill its juice.

Oysters Rockefeller

 **1 hour**

Classic, old-school New Orleans flavor, slightly updated. Because of the expense of the oysters, these are better for smaller crowds, 10 to 12 people max.

Makes 24 pieces

6 tablespoons unsalted butter

2 garlic cloves, minced

½ cup panko (Japanese bread crumbs)

2 shallots, chopped

2 pounds fresh spinach, stemmed and chopped

Sea salt and freshly ground black pepper

¼ cup Pernod

Tabasco sauce

Extra-virgin olive oil

¼ cup grated Parmigiano-Reggiano cheese

2 tablespoons chopped fresh flat-leaf parsley

24 oysters

3 pounds coarse sea salt or kosher salt

Lemon wedges, for garnish

Preheat the oven to 450°F. Melt 4 tablespoons of the butter in a skillet over medium-low heat. Sauté the garlic for 2 minutes to infuse the butter. Place the bread crumbs in a mixing bowl and pour in half of the garlic butter to moisten them; set aside. Add the shallots to the garlic butter remaining in the skillet and cook for 3 minutes, until soft. Add the spinach and cook until it is wilted and the water in the spinach has evaporated; season with salt and pepper. Pour in the Pernod and cook down for a few minutes until the mixture is dry and then add a couple of dashes of Tabasco to give the spinach a little kick. Take the pan off the heat and stir in the remaining 2 tablespoons of butter. Finish off the bread crumbs by mixing in a 2-count of olive oil, the Parmigiano, and the parsley; season with salt and pepper. Set the bread crumb mixture aside.

Shuck the oysters (see sidebar, opposite). Spread a thick, even layer of the salt on a baking pan. Spoon 1 heaping teaspoon of the spinach mixture onto each oyster, followed by a spoonful of the garlic bread crumbs. Nestle the oysters in the salt to steady them. Bake for 15 minutes or until the bread crumbs brown. Serve with lemon wedges and Tabasco sauce.

Raw Oysters with Bloody Mary Cocktail Sauce

 **15 minutes**

You can't argue with tradition, but you can update it. The cocktail sauce is also great with cold poached shrimp.

Makes 24 pieces ★ Makes 3 cups sauce

Cocktail Sauce

½ cup ketchup

1 ripe tomato, coarsely chopped

1 celery stalk, coarsely chopped

½ onion, coarsely chopped

2 tablespoons grated fresh or prepared horseradish

Juice of 1 lemon

2 teaspoons Tabasco sauce

1 tablespoon Worcestershire sauce

1 shot pepper vodka

1 teaspoon celery seed

Sea salt and freshly ground black pepper

24 oysters

¼ cup chopped celery leaves, for garnish

¼ cup minced fresh chives, for garnish

Combine the cocktail sauce ingredients in a blender and blend until smooth. Shuck the oysters according to the sidebar on page 220. Spoon the cocktail sauce over the raw oysters on the half shell. Garnish with the chopped celery leaves and chives.

Raw Oysters with Leek, Tomato, and Bacon Vinaigrette

 **30 minutes**

This vinaigrette is more like a chunky sauce, and is also great as a topping for bread toasts. Don't refrigerate the vinaigrette—the fat from the bacon turns from liquid to solid.

Makes 24 pieces ✳ Makes 2½ cups vinaigrette

2 tomatoes
4 bacon slices
2 leeks, white part only, trimmed, washed, and minced
2 tablespoons balsamic vinegar
Pinch of sugar
2 tablespoons chopped fresh flat-leaf parsley
Sea salt and freshly ground black pepper
24 oysters

Bring a small pot of lightly salted water to a boil. With a sharp paring knife, cut out the tough cores from each tomato. Make a small X in the bottom of each to make peeling easier. Drop the tomatoes in the boiling water and count to 20. Remove the tomatoes with a slotted spoon and run them under cool water. Peel off the skins with the paring knife. Cut the tomatoes in half and gently squeeze out the seeds. Dice the tomatoes and set aside.

Fry the bacon in a skillet over medium-low heat until crisp. Remove to a paper towel to drain. Sauté the leeks in the bacon fat until tender. Put the leeks into a bowl and fold in the tomatoes, vinegar, sugar, and parsley; season with salt and pepper. Shuck the oysters according to the sidebar on page 220. Spoon some of the vinaigrette onto each oyster, crumble the bacon on top, and serve.

*Cocktails

Mixed drinks served in great-looking glasses can really help create a festive mood at a party, but providing a full bar can be tricky (and expensive) to pull off if you need to lay in a big variety of mixers and liqueurs.

Instead, I generally serve beer and wine, plus one special "cocktail of the evening" that fits well with the atmosphere I'm going for. I start by assessing my crowd and the mood for the event: Martinis might be appropriate for a quieter, more sophisticated event, while a mojito, woo woo, or sangría would get things going at a casual or outdoor affair. I like to mix up a big batch of my chosen cocktail in a large pitcher and let the guests serve themselves so no one gets stuck doing bartender duty all night.

Cuban Mojito

You can also make these in a pitcher and serve them as the evening's party drink. They have the perfect balance of tart and sweet. Great in the summer.

Serves 2

1 lime, cut in wedges ★ ½ cup sugar ★ Handful fresh mint, plus more for garnish ★ ½ cup light rum ★ Soda water ★ 2 pieces fresh sugar-cane stalks (optional)

In a martini shaker or wide glass, combine the lime, sugar, and mint. Using a muddler or the handle of a wooden spoon, smash and crush everything together to release the oils and juice from the lime rind and mint leaves. When you have some nice juice in there and the sugar begins to dissolve, add the rum and stir it around to combine. Fill 2 glasses with ice, divide the mixture between the glasses, and top off with some soda. Garnish with a couple of mint leaves. For extra pizzazz stick a piece of sugarcane in the glass to use as a stirrer.

Pineapple Mimosa

Serves 2

Champagne, chilled ★ ¼ cup pineapple juice

Pour the champagne into 2 glasses and top with the pineapple juice.

Woo Woo

This orange, peach, cranberry, and lime drink makes the ultimate "fruit cocktail."

Serves a party

1 (14 liter) bottle mandarin orange vodka ★ ½ cup peach schnapps ★ 1 quart cranberry juice ★ Juice of 2 limes

In a large pitcher, mix together all the ingredients with some ice. Pour into highball glasses and serve.

Sangría Blanca

Serves a party

4 bottles dry white wine, such as sauvignon blanc ★
1 cup Spanish sherry ★ 1 cup Cointreau ★ ½ cup sugar
★ 1 bunch seedless white grapes ★ 3 lemons, unpeeled and
sliced ★ 3 white peaches, pitted and sliced, with skin
★ 1 honeydew melon, peeled and sliced ★ 1 liter club soda

Combine everything except the club soda in a large pitcher or
punch bowl. Give it a stir. Let the flavors blend for several hours.
Before serving, add the club soda and some ice.

Lemon-Ginger Ice

Serves 2

½ cup tequila ★ ¼ cup Triple Sec ★ Juice of 1 lemon
★ 1 tablespoon freshly grated ginger ★ 1 cup ice cubes

Combine all ingredients in a blender. Blend to a
smoothie-like consistency.

Martini Noir

*This drink is a twist on the dirty martini using black olives instead
of green. James Bond mastered the mystique of the martini—it is
the ultimate sexy drink. The icy vodka, the dryness of the vermouth,
and the salty olives make the ultimate* ménage à trois.

Serves 2

½ cup vodka or gin ★ 1 teaspoon dry vermouth ★ 1 tablespoon
olive juice from the kalamata olives ★ 6 kalamata olives

Combine the vodka, vermouth, and olive juice in a shaker with ice.
Shake it up really well to break up the ice into shards. Strain into 2
martini glasses and garnish each drink with 3 black olives. Poke the
olives with toothpicks as if you're bobbing for apples.

Apple Martini

Serves 2

½ cup vodka ★ ¼ cup apple juice ★ ¼ cup apple schnapps, such as Apple Pucker ★ A few paper-thin slices of Granny Smith apples, for garnish

Combine the vodka, apple juice, and apple schnapps in a shaker with ice. Shake it up really well to break up the ice into shards. Strain into 2 martini glasses and garnish each drink with a slice of apple.

Orange Sidecar

Serves 2

½ cup brandy ★ 2 tablespoons Triple Sec ★ 3 tablespoons freshly squeezed lemon juice ★ 3 tablespoons orange juice

Combine all the ingredients in a shaker with ice. Shake well and strain into a couple of cocktail glasses.

Manhattan Sunrise

Serves 2

½ cup bourbon, Maker's Mark preferred ★ 2 tablespoons sweet vermouth ★ 2 dashes bitters ★ Splash of orange juice ★ 2 tablespoons Chambord ★ 4 maraschino cherries

Combine the bourbon, vermouth, bitters, and OJ in a shaker. Shake it up and pour into 2 highball glasses filled with ice. Add the Chambord by tilting the glass and slowly pouring it down the side of the glass (as you would a beer). The Chambord should go straight to the bottom and then rise up slowly through the drink. Garnish each drink with a couple of cherries.

Happy Ending

Serves 2

2 shots brewed espresso, cooled * ¼ cup half-and-half *
¼ cup Frangelico * ¼ cup Grand Marnier * Cocoa powder, for dusting

Combine the espresso, half-and-half, Frangelico, and Grand
Marnier in a shaker with ice. Shake well and pour into a
couple of glasses filled with ice. Dust with cocoa powder.

Moist Towelette

Serves 2

½ cup gin * 2 tablespoons blue curaçao * 2 tablespoons
Triple Sec * Juice of 1 lime * ¼ cup soda water

Combine all the ingredients in a shaker with ice. Shake well
and strain into a couple of martini glasses.

Green Tea Sake

Serves 4

1 cup water * 2 green tea bags * ¼ cup sugar * 1 pint sake, chilled

Bring the water to a boil in a pot, add the tea bags, shut off the heat, and
let steep for 2 minutes. Squeeze out the tea bags and discard them. Add
the sugar to the brewed tea and swirl it around so it dissolves. Chill the
green tea syrup until cold. Mix the sake with the simple syrup and pour
it into sake cups.

a little on the side

Chefs know that when people order in restaurants, they choose their entrée by the side dish that accompanies it. Hence, the popularity of the question "What does that come with?" But a better question is, "What does the side dish bring to the plate?" Consider: What is a steak without mashed potatoes? What is turkey without stuffing? You get the point. Side dishes make the world go round.

People love their sides, no doubt about it, but there's more to life than a baked potato or a sad little green salad. Whether we are going back to my roots for some intensely flavorful corn pudding, collard greens, or black-eyed peas, or exploring world flavors like sesame and curry, the side dishes in this chapter more than hold their own on the plate and make the entire meal just that much more spectacular.

Slow-Roasted
Plum Tomatoes

 3¼ hours

These sweet roasted tomatoes are great on sandwiches or chopped up in pasta.

Serves 4 to 6

8 plum tomatoes
Extra-virgin olive oil
4 garlic cloves, sliced
½ bunch fresh thyme
Sea salt and freshly ground black pepper

Preheat the oven to 300°F. Slice the tomatoes in half lengthwise and put them in a large bowl. Drizzle with a 4-count of oil. Toss in the garlic and thyme; season with salt and pepper. Toss the tomatoes to coat in the flavored oil. Arrange the tomatoes on a sheet pan in a single layer, cut side up. Pour the oil from the bowl over the tomatoes and roast for 3 hours to concentrate their flavor. They should be shrunken and dry to the touch.

Corn Pudding

 1½ **hours**

Corn pudding is deliciously simple to put together.

Serves 6

2 ears fresh corn in their husks
2 cups milk
½ cup heavy cream
2 tablespoons unsalted butter
¾ cup yellow cornmeal
3 tablespoons chopped fresh chives
Sea salt and freshly ground black pepper
3 eggs, separated

Preheat the oven to 350°F. Put the 2 ears of corn, in the husks, in the oven, directly on the center rack. Roast the corn for 30 minutes, until soft. Cool slightly so you don't burn your hands and then remove the husks. Cut the kernels off the cob with a sharp knife and set the loose corn aside. Leave the oven on.

In a large pot over low heat, combine the milk, cream, and butter. Once the butter has melted, turn up the heat slightly and bring the mixture to just under a boil. Pour in the cornmeal in a slow steady stream, whisking at the same time. Cook and whisk constantly until the cornmeal is blended in and the mixture is smooth and thick; it should look like porridge. Take the pot off the stove and fold in the corn, chives, and salt and pepper. Mix in the egg yolks, one at a time, to make it more like a batter. In a separate bowl, beat the egg whites (use a hand blender if you have one) until they hold stiff peaks. Fold the whites into the corn pudding to lighten it. Coat the bottom and sides of an 8 × 8-inch baking dish with nonstick spray. Spoon the batter into the prepared baking dish and bake for 25 to 30 minutes. When it's done, the corn pudding will look puffed and golden brown, like a soufflé.

Garlic-Chive Mashed Potatoes

 **45 minutes**

Serves 6

1 head garlic
2 pounds Yukon Gold potatoes, peeled and quartered
1 tablespoon sea salt
1 cup heavy cream (see Note)
½ cup (1 stick) unsalted butter
Sea salt and freshly ground black pepper
2 tablespoons chopped fresh chives

Bang the garlic on the counter to break up the cloves; then peel off the skins. Put the garlic and potatoes in a large pot and cover with cold water. Add the salt and bring to a boil, uncovered. Simmer until there is no resistance when a fork is inserted into the potatoes, about 30 minutes. While that's going, warm the heavy cream and butter in a small pot over low heat until the butter is melted.

Drain the potatoes and garlic well in a colander and then put them in a large bowl. While the potatoes are still hot, pour in the warm cream and pulverize the potatoes with a potato masher. Season with salt and pepper; sprinkle with chives before serving.

Note: *If you plan on holding the mashed potatoes for a little bit, add an extra ½ cup of warm heavy cream so the potatoes will soak up the moisture and remain fluffy.*

Braised Red Cabbage with Apples and Dill

 **45 minutes**

Serves 4 to 6

1 head red cabbage, about 2 pounds
2 tablespoons unsalted butter
1 onion, sliced
2 Granny Smith apples, cored, peeled, and sliced
1 tablespoon chopped fresh dill, plus more for garnish
2 bay leaves
½ teaspoon caraway seed
½ cup Chicken Stock (page 156)
⅓ cup cider vinegar
3 tablespoons sugar
Sea salt and freshly ground black pepper

Quarter the cabbage and cut out the core; then cut the quarters into thirds. Rinse the cabbage in cold water and set aside. In a large stockpot, melt the butter over medium heat. Sauté the onion and apples for 2 minutes, until they begin to soften. Add the cabbage, dill, bay leaves, caraway, and stock and cook for 5 minutes, until the cabbage begins to wilt. Stir in the vinegar to preserve the red color. Add sugar, salt, and pepper and cook for 20 minutes or until the cabbage is soft, stirring occasionally. Garnish with chopped dill before serving.

Perfect Steamed Jasmine Rice

 **30 minutes**

In my experience, many people have trouble cooking rice. It's a dish that seems so simple but can baffle the most adept cook. Follow this straightforward recipe and success will be yours.

Serves 4 ★ Makes 3½ cups

1 cup jasmine rice
2 cups water
1½ teaspoons sea salt
Unsalted butter (optional)

Rinse the rice in a colander until the water runs clear to remove some of the starch. Let the rice drain. Put the rice, water, and salt in a medium pot and place over medium heat. When the water begins to boil, stir it once; then cover tightly and lower the heat. Simmer the rice for 15 minutes without lifting the lid—it is wise to set a timer. After 15 minutes take the cover off to check the rice. The water should be absorbed and the rice cooked but firm. Fluff the cooked grains with a fork so they separate. Do not stir it with a spoon or the rice will become gummy. Add a little butter if you like.

White Cheddar Macaroni and Cheese

  **1 hour**

Serves 6

1 pound elbow macaroni
3 tablespoons unsalted butter
3 tablespoons all-purpose flour
3 cups milk
4 cups shredded sharp white Cheddar cheese, plus 1 cup for the top
Sea salt and freshly ground black pepper

Cook the macaroni in lightly salted boiling water for about 10 minutes, until tender but still firm. Drain well and set aside.

Preheat the oven to 400°F. In a deep skillet, melt the butter over medium heat. Add the flour to make a roux and cook, stirring constantly, to remove any lumps. Pour in the milk and cook until the mixture is thick and smooth, still stirring all the while. Stir in 4 cups of the Cheddar and continue to cook and stir until the cheese melts. Season with salt and pepper. Add the cooked macaroni and fold to incorporate. Transfer the macaroni mixture to a 3-quart baking dish. Sprinkle the top with the remaining cup of shredded cheese. Bake for 30 minutes, until hot and bubbly.

Braised Leeks with Smoked Bacon and Tomato

 **45 minutes**

Small leeks are essential for this dish.

Serves 4 to 6

6 small leeks
Extra-virgin olive oil
2 bacon strips, cut in small pieces
2 garlic cloves, minced
Leaves from 4 fresh thyme sprigs
1 (28-ounce) can whole tomatoes, hand-crushed
Sea salt and freshly ground black pepper

Preheat the oven to 350°F. Trim the root off the end of the leeks and cut off all but 1 inch of the green part. Halve the leeks lengthwise. Rinse really well under cool water, checking for dirt everywhere; it gets trapped in all the outer layers. Heat a large ovenproof skillet over medium heat and drizzle with a 2-count of olive oil. Add the bacon and cook for 5 minutes to render down the fat. Add the garlic and thyme and give it a stir. Arrange the leeks side by side in the pan and pour the tomatoes on top. Season with salt and pepper, cover, and bake for 30 minutes.

Soft Polenta with Parmesan and Black Pepper

 **45 minutes**

Serves 6

2 quarts Chicken Stock (page 156)

1 teaspoon sea salt

2 cups polenta or yellow cornmeal

⅓ cup heavy cream

2 tablespoons unsalted butter, at room temperature

1 cup freshly grated Parmigiano-Reggiano cheese

1½ teaspoons freshly ground black pepper

In a large pot, bring the chicken stock and salt to a boil. Gradually whisk in the cornmeal in a slow, steady stream. The liquid will be absorbed and the cornmeal will lock up; don't freak, just whisk through it. Lower the heat and continue to whisk until the polenta is thick and smooth, about 20 minutes. Add the cream and butter; continue to stir until incorporated, about 10 minutes. Remove from the heat, fold in the Parmigiano and black pepper, and serve.

Cranberry Conserve with Oranges and Walnuts

 **1 hour**

This tart treat is welcome on any Thanksgiving table.

Serves 6 to 8 ★ **Makes 4 cups**

1 quart unfiltered cranberry juice

¼ cup apple cider

2 cups sugar

Peel of 1 orange, cut in large strips

1 tablespoon grated ginger

1 cup walnuts, toasted and coarsely chopped

1 tablespoon balsamic vinegar

1 pound fresh cranberries

In a medium saucepan over high heat, combine the cranberry juice, apple cider, sugar, orange peel, and ginger. Boil until the mixture is reduced by half, about 20 minutes. Add the walnuts, vinegar, and cranberries. Bring back up to a boil and continue to cook, stirring often, until the cranberries burst, about 20 minutes.

Grilled Peaches with Rosemary and Balsamic

 **20 minutes**

Photo on page 230

Serves 4 to 6

¼ cup extra-virgin olive oil, plus extra for greasing the grill
4 peaches, halved and pitted
2 tablespoons balsamic vinegar
Needles from 2 fresh rosemary sprigs
Sea salt and freshly ground black pepper

Preheat a grill or grill pan until hot. Wipe the grates (or the ridges of your pan) with oil to keep the peaches from sticking. Toss all the ingredients together in a bowl until the peaches are well coated. Put the peaches cut side down on the grill and cook for 5 to 8 minutes, until the flesh of the peaches softens slightly and caramelizes. Turn the peaches over with tongs and grill the other sides for 3 to 5 minutes to char the skin. That's summer love.

Collard Greens
with Ham Hocks and Garlic

 **2 hours**

Serves 4 to 6

4 pounds young collard greens, about 4 bunches
3 tablespoons extra-virgin olive oil
1 onion, sliced thin
2 garlic cloves, smashed
2 large smoked ham hocks, about 2 pounds
2 bay leaves
2 quarts Chicken Stock (page 156)
¼ cup apple cider vinegar
1 tablespoon sugar
1 teaspoon red pepper flakes
Lawry's Seasoned Salt, to taste

To prepare the greens, cut away the tough stalks and stems from the collards and discard any leaves that are bruised or yellow. Fill the sink with water and salt (the salt helps to remove any impurities) and wash the collards thoroughly to remove any grit. Repeat 2 or 3 times until the water runs clear. Dry the greens thoroughly. Stack up several leaves and hand-shred them into ribbonlike pieces. Repeat until all the leaves are shredded.

Coat a 6-quart stockpot with the olive oil and place it over medium heat. Add the onion and garlic, stir to coat, and add the ham hocks and bay leaves; cook about 8 minutes. Pack in the greens, pushing them down into the pot; then add the stock, vinegar, sugar, and red pepper flakes. Bring up to a hard boil for 10 minutes, until the greens start to wilt. Turn the greens over with a wooden spoon. Lower to a gentle boil, cover the pot, and cook for 45 minutes. Taste the pot liquor (broth) and check the seasoning, adding seasoned salt to your taste. Cover and cook for 15 more minutes.

Butternut Squash Soufflé

 **1½ hours**

Great for holidays. Even good as a dessert.

Serves 4

Preheat the oven to 350°F. Halve the butternut squash lengthwise and remove the seeds and strings.

1 butternut squash, about 2 pounds

Extra-virgin olive oil

Sea salt and freshly ground black pepper

Zest of 1 orange, finely grated

½ teaspoon minced fresh rosemary

1 teaspoon ground cinnamon

2 tablespoons unsalted butter, at room temperature, plus more for greasing the soufflé dish

4 eggs, separated

Pinch of cream of tartar

Granulated sugar, for the soufflé dish

Confectioners' sugar, for dusting

Brush the insides with oil; season with salt and pepper. Turn the squash over and place the halves side by side on a rack in a roasting pan, cut side down. Bake for 45 minutes, until fork-tender.

Remove the squash from the oven, scoop out the flesh, and put it in a food processor; you should have 2 cups. Add the orange zest, rosemary, cinnamon, and butter and season with salt and pepper. Pulse to combine. Scrape the butternut squash puree into a bowl and cool to room temperature. Whisk in the egg yolks to cream out the filling.

In a separate clean bowl beat the egg whites and cream of tartar to stiff peaks. With a rubber spatula, fold one third of the beaten whites into the squash mixture to lighten it. Then gently fold in the rest.

Grease a 2-quart soufflé dish with softened butter, sprinkle with granulated sugar, and pour out any excess. (The butter and sugar will keep the soufflé from sticking to the sides, allowing it to rise evenly.) Spoon the butternut squash mixture into the prepared baking dish and place on a cookie sheet. Bake on the middle oven rack for about 30 minutes. The soufflé is done when it has puffed over the rim, the outside is golden, and the center jiggles slightly. Dust with confectioners' sugar before serving.

Creamed Spinach with Nutmeg

 **20 minutes**

Serves 4 to 6

Extra-virgin olive oil
1 tablespoon unsalted butter
1 onion, minced
2 garlic cloves, minced
2 pounds fresh spinach, stemmed
½ cup heavy cream
½ teaspoon grated fresh nutmeg
Sea salt and freshly ground black pepper

Heat a large pot over medium heat. Drizzle with a 2-count of oil, add the butter, and stir it around so it melts. Sauté the onion and garlic until soft, about 5 minutes. Add the spinach in batches, pushing it down with a wooden spoon to help it wilt. Keep adding more spinach when there is room in the pot. Cook the spinach until it is dry, then lower the heat and add the cream and nutmeg. Stir and cook for 10 minutes. Season with salt and pepper and serve hot.

Chilled Asparagus with Citrus Vinaigrette

 15 minutes

Serves 4 to 6

2 bunches asparagus, trimmed
Juice and zest of 1 orange
Juice and zest of 1 lime
Juice and zest of 1 lemon
1 tablespoon Dijon mustard
Sea salt and freshly ground black pepper
¼ cup canola oil
Fresh mint, for garnish

Bring a pot of lightly salted water to a boil and fill a large bowl with ice water. Trim off the woody ends of the spears. Blanch the asparagus in the boiling water for 3 minutes. Dump the asparagus in the ice water to stop them from overcooking and getting mushy. This also keeps the bright green color.

Whiz the citrus juices, zests, mustard, salt, and pepper together in a blender. Gradually drizzle in the oil until the vinaigrette thickens. Drain the asparagus and arrange the spears on a serving platter. Pour on the vinaigrette, garnish with fresh mint, and we're home. *I added honey*

Black-Eyed Peas with Stewed Tomatoes and Chile

 1¼ **hours**

In this dish a hunk of ham is left whole as it cooks with the peas. Not cutting it up is very country.

Serves 4 to 6

Extra-virgin olive oil
3 garlic cloves, smashed
1 fresh green chile, halved
1 piece country ham, about 4 ounces
1 pound dried black-eyed peas
2 bay leaves
2 quarts Chicken Stock (page 156)
Sea salt and freshly ground black pepper
1 (28-ounce) can whole tomatoes, hand-crushed
¼ cup sugar

Place a 2-gallon stockpot over medium heat. Drizzle with a 2-count of oil. Sauté the garlic, green chile, and country ham together until the garlic is soft, about 3 minutes. Add the black-eyed peas, bay leaves, and chicken stock. Simmer for 45 minutes, until the beans are tender, stirring when you think about it. Wait until halfway through the cooking process to begin seasoning with salt and pepper. You want the flesh of the bean to break down a little bit first so the flavors can penetrate the beans.

In a separate pan, cook the tomatoes and sugar over medium-low heat for 20 minutes, stirring occasionally, until the tomatoes are like jam. Serve the black-eyed peas in a large bowl and spoon the sweet tomatoes on top.

Salt-and-Herb–Roasted New Potatoes

 45 minutes

Serves 4 to 6

2 pounds red new potatoes
¼ cup extra-virgin olive oil
1 tablespoon fresh rosemary needles
Leaves from ¼ bunch fresh thyme
¼ cup sea salt

Preheat the oven to 375°F. Toss everything together in a large bowl. Dump the herbed potatoes on a baking sheet and spread them out in a single layer. Pour any remaining oil on top. Bake for 30 to 40 minutes, until the potatoes are cooked through and crispy around the edges.

Roasted Carrots
with Orange Brown Butter
and Sage

 **45 minutes**

This is the color of autumn.

Serves 4

1 bunch young carrots, with tops
¼ cup extra-virgin olive oil
Sea salt and freshly ground black pepper
4 tablespoons (½ stick) unsalted butter
1 orange, halved
1 tablespoon brown sugar
4 sage leaves

Preheat the oven to 350°F. Cut off all but 1 inch of the carrot tops, leaving a little green. Put the carrots in a large shallow pan, add the oil, and season with salt and pepper. Turn to coat the carrots. Stick them in the oven and bake for 30 minutes, until the carrots are fork-tender.

In the meantime, melt the butter in a skillet over medium-low heat. Swirl the pan around and cook until the butter begins to become brown and nutty—crazy nutty. Squeeze in the juice from the orange halves, add the brown sugar and sage, and continue to cook for 2 minutes or until syrupy.

Remove the carrots from the oven and arrange them on a platter. Drizzle the orange brown butter over the carrots and serve.

Roasted Sweet Potatoes with Miso, Orange, and Sesame

 **45 minutes**

Serves 4

6 small sweet potatoes
1 cup orange juice
1 cup water
1-inch piece of fresh ginger, whacked with the flat side of a knife
1 tablespoon light miso
1 tablespoon low-sodium soy sauce
1 garlic clove, halved
1 tablespoon brown sugar
1 tablespoon sesame seeds

Preheat the oven to 350°F. Pierce the sweet potatoes with a fork and bake until tender, 30 to 40 minutes. While they're baking, make the sauce. In a saucepan over medium-low heat, combine the orange juice, water, ginger, miso, soy sauce, garlic, and brown sugar. Cook until the sauce reduces and is thick enough to coat the back of a spoon, about 15 minutes. Set aside.

When the sweet potatoes are cool enough to touch, slice them in half lengthwise and lay them face up on a sheet pan. Spoon the sauce over the flesh of the potatoes, sprinkle with the sesame seeds, and broil until the sesame seeds are toasted.

Red Onions Roasted with Balsamic and Honey

 **45 minutes**

Very unpretentious and delicious. There's no need to trim the onion roots; the dish looks more rustic with them as is.

Serves 4 to 6

¼ cup extra-virgin olive oil
2 tablespoons balsamic vinegar
⅓ cup honey
½ bunch fresh thyme
Sea salt and freshly ground black pepper
3 red onions, unpeeled, halved lengthwise

Preheat the oven to 375°F. In a small bowl, whisk together the oil, vinegar, honey, thyme, salt, and pepper until combined. Put the onions in a large bowl and pour the dressing over them. Toss everything together until the onions are well coated. Put the onions on a sheet pan, cut side up, and bake for 40 minutes, until the onions are soft and slightly caramelized.

Green Beans with Caramelized Shallots and Walnuts

 20 minutes

Serves 4 to 6

1 pound green beans
Extra-virgin olive oil
2 shallots, cut in circles
½ cup walnuts
Sea salt and freshly ground black pepper
Juice of ½ lemon
2 tablespoons chopped fresh flat-leaf parsley

Bring a pot of slightly salted water to a boil. Blanch the green beans in the boiling water for 3 minutes; drain and set aside. Put a skillet over medium heat and add a 3-count of oil. Sauté the shallots for 3 minutes, stirring frequently, until they begin to soften and get some color. Add the walnuts and cook for 3 more minutes, tossing frequently, until the nuts get toasty. Add the green beans; season with salt and pepper. Toss it all together; then give a squeeze of lemon juice and hit it with the parsley. It's good, tasty, and simple.

Baked Eggplant with Sesame Yogurt and Mint

 45 minutes

The eggplant is also great grilled. The yogurt sauce is my version of tahini.

Serves 4 to 6

6 Japanese eggplants, halved lengthwise
Extra-virgin olive oil
1 fresh red chile, thinly sliced on the diagonal
Sea salt and freshly ground black pepper
½ cup plain yogurt
¼ cup sesame seeds, toasted, plus more for garnish (see Note, page 34)
Juice of ½ lemon
Fresh mint, for garnish

Preheat the oven to 450°F. Put the eggplant in a large shallow bowl and add the oil, chile, salt, and pepper. Toss to coat. Arrange the eggplant on a sheet pan, cut side down, and bake for 40 minutes, until soft. While the eggplant is in the oven, make the yogurt sauce.

Combine the yogurt, sesame seeds, and lemon juice in a food processor or blender; doesn't matter. Blend until creamy and smooth. Season with salt and pepper. When the hot, gooey, sticky eggplant comes out of the oven, drizzle the yogurt sauce on top and garnish with more sesame seeds and some fresh mint. Nice Moroccan dish.

Caramelized Endive with Anchovy Butter

 **25 minutes**

Serves 4

4 endives, halved lengthwise
Extra-virgin olive oil
2 garlic cloves, minced
2 anchovy fillets, minced
Sea salt and freshly ground black pepper
4 tablespoons (½ stick) unsalted butter, at room temperature
Juice of ½ lemon

Place a skillet over low heat and drizzle with a 3-count of oil. Arrange the endives, cut side down, in the skillet, cover, and cook for 15 to 20 minutes, or until the endives get mushy. While they're doing their thing, combine the garlic, anchovies, a pinch of salt, and the butter in a small bowl and mash them with a fork until combined. Turn the endive cut side up and top each with a spoonful of butter. Just let it melt. Give a squeeze of lemon, season with salt and pepper, and that's it.

Corn Roasted in Its Own Jacket

 **40 minutes**

Boiling corn leaches out all the flavor and natural sweetness. Once you try corn this way, you will never look back.

Serves 4

4 ears fresh corn, unhusked

Preheat the oven to 350°F. Place the corn in its husks directly on the oven rack and roast for 30 to 40 minutes, until the corn is soft when you press on it. Peel down the husks and tie in a knot to use as a handle when eating. This method produces by far the sweetest corn I have ever had.

Potato Gratin

 **1 hour**

Slice the potatoes right before you assemble the dish so they don't turn brown.

Serves 6

2 pounds baking potatoes, peeled and sliced paper-thin

2 cups heavy cream

2 garlic cloves, split

Leaves from 4 fresh thyme sprigs

3 tablespoons chopped fresh chives, plus more for garnish

1 cup grated Parmigiano-Reggiano cheese

Sea salt and freshly ground black pepper

Preheat the oven to 375°F. In a large bowl combine all the ingredients, tossing to coat. Season with salt and pepper. Put the potato mixture into a casserole dish, flatten it out with a spatula, and bake for 40 minutes, until the potatoes are tender and the gratin is bubbly. Let stand for 10 minutes before serving. Garnish with fresh chives. This is comfort food at its finest!

Mushrooms Sautéed with Garlic, Ginger, and Soy

 **20 minutes**

Fish is my fave thing to serve with this.

Serves 4

¼ cup sesame oil
2 garlic cloves, halved
1-inch piece ginger, whacked open with the flat side of a knife
2 pounds assorted mushrooms, your choice
¼ cup low-sodium soy sauce
1 tablespoon brown sugar
Pinch of red pepper flakes

Place a skillet over medium heat and add the sesame oil, garlic, and ginger. Add the mushrooms and cook and stir for 8 to 10 minutes, or until the mushrooms begin to caramelize. Add the soy sauce and then sprinkle with the sugar. Continue to cook for 3 to 5 minutes to dissolve the sugar. Add the red pepper flakes and serve.

Slow-Cooked Squash with Fresh Thyme, Parmigiano, and Olive Oil

 45 minutes

Serves 4

4 yellow summer squash, cut in circles

¼ cup extra-virgin olive oil

Sea salt and freshly ground black pepper

Leaves from 3 fresh thyme sprigs

½ cup grated Parmigiano-Reggiano cheese

1 cup panko (Japanese bread crumbs)

½ cup (1 stick) unsalted butter, melted, for top

Preheat the oven to 350°F. Toss the squash in a bowl with the oil, salt, pepper, thyme, cheese, and bread crumbs. Put the mixture in a casserole dish and drizzle with the melted butter. Bake for 40 minutes, until golden brown and bubbly.

sweet
tooth

I like very homey desserts that make your lips quiver with satisfaction. You don't have to be a pastry chef to master these; all you need is a sweet tooth and a passion for warm, bright, gooey flavors that never go out of style. A few mixing bowls, a couple of standard baking pans, and that's it: perfect desserts like Triple Chocolate Threat, the only birthday cake recipe you'll ever need, or Cheesecake so rich and creamy you'll swear you're in Brooklyn. Basically what I'm saying is save room for dessert.

Ginger Spice Cake

 **2 hours**

Here is a fantastic coffee cake that tastes like gingerbread: perfect for cold days or nights.

Serves 8

Ginger Spice Cake

2 cups all-purpose flour

1 teaspoon baking soda

1 tablespoon ground ginger

2 teaspoons ground cinnamon

½ teaspoon ground cloves

½ teaspoon allspice

1 egg

½ cup molasses

1 cup sugar

½ cup unsalted butter, melted

1 cup buttermilk

Warm Cranberries

2 cups fresh cranberries

1 cup dried cranberries

2 cups water

2 cups brown sugar, packed

1 teaspoon allspice

½ teaspoon freshly grated nutmeg

1 cup whipped cream, for garnish

Preheat the oven to 350°F. Coat a 9-inch round cake pan with nonstick cooking spray. Cut a circle of parchment paper to fit the pan bottom and place it inside; then spray the paper. Set aside.

Sift the dry ingredients into a large bowl. In the bowl of an electric mixer, beat the egg, molasses, sugar, and melted butter until thick. Gradually mix in the dry ingredients in 3 batches, alternating with the buttermilk. Beat for 1 minute after each addition to incorporate the ingredients and strengthen the cake's structure. Mix until the batter is smooth.

Pour the batter into the prepared cake pan and smooth down the top of the batter until even. Bake for 35 to 40 minutes or until a wooden toothpick inserted into the middle of the cake comes out clean.

While the cake is baking, combine the ingredients for the cranberries in a large pot. Bring to a boil over medium heat. Simmer for 20 minutes, stirring occasionally. Allow the cake to cool completely before removing it from the pan, then slice it in wedges. Serve with the cranberries and whipped cream.

Blueberry-Lemon Tart

 **1½ hours**

Photo on page 270

Lemon and blueberry are a perfect pair, like Bert and Ernie. You will need a 10½-inch tart pan with a removable bottom. Serve this year round.

Serves 6 to 8

Pastry

1½ cups all-purpose flour

2 tablespoons sugar

Pinch of salt

½ cup (1 stick) unsalted butter, cold, in chunks

1 egg, separated

2 tablespoons ice water

Filling

4 eggs

1½ cups sugar

¼ cup heavy cream

1 cup fresh lemon juice, about 5 lemons

Zest of 1 lemon

1 pint blueberries

To make the pastry, pulse the flour, sugar, and salt together in a food processor. Put in the chunks of butter, a little at a time, and pulse just until the dough resembles cornmeal. Add the egg yolk and the ice water; pulse again for a second just to pull the dough together. Wrap the dough tightly in plastic and let it rest and chill in the refrigerator for 30 minutes.

Preheat the oven to 350°F. Using a rolling pin, roll the dough out on a lightly floured surface to a 12-inch circle. Carefully roll the dough up onto the pin (this may take a little practice) and lay it inside a 10½-inch tart pan with a removable bottom. Press the dough into the scalloped edges of the pan and fold the excess dough inside to reinforce the rim.

Put the tart pan on a cookie sheet and prick the bottom of the dough with a fork. Bake for 20 minutes. Lightly beat the egg white and brush the bottom and sides of the dough with it to seal any tiny holes. Bake for another 10 minutes.

To make the lemon curd filling, whisk together the eggs, sugar, heavy cream, lemon juice, and zest. Pour the mixture into the tart shell. Spread the blueberries on top of the filling; they will float around and find their own space. Bake for 20 to 25 minutes. The curd will jiggle slightly when done. Carefully lift the tart out of the ring, then slide it off the base onto a plate. Cool to room temperature and slice.

Espresso Pots de Crème with Pistachio Biscotti

 >¶○| **2 hours + chilling time**

You will need ramekins to make this recipe. The pots de crème taste like coffee pudding. Both can be made a day in advance. Store the cookies in an airtight container.

Serves 6 ★ Makes 24 cookies

Espresso Pots de Crème

3 cups heavy cream
½ teaspoon vanilla extract
¼ cup whole black coffee beans
6 egg yolks
½ cup sugar
3 tablespoons brewed espresso coffee, cold

Pistachio Biscotti

½ cup (1 stick) unsalted butter
3 eggs
1 cup sugar
1 teaspoon vanilla extract
3½ cups all-purpose flour
1 teaspoon baking powder
½ teaspoon salt
1½ cups pistachios, toasted (see page 206)

Pour the heavy cream, vanilla, and coffee beans into a saucepan and place over medium-low heat. Bring the cream to a brief simmer; do not boil or it will overflow within seconds. Remove from heat and strain to remove the beans.

In a large bowl, whisk together the egg yolks and the sugar until the color turns light yellow, about 3 minutes. Temper the yolks by very gradually whisking the hot cream into the yolk and sugar mixture (do not add the hot cream too quickly or the eggs will cook). Stir in the brewed coffee.

>>

Preheat the oven to 325°F. Pour the egg-cream mixture into six 8-ounce ramekins, filling them three-quarters of the way full with the mixture. Fill a large, shallow baking pan with ½ inch of hot water. Carefully place the ramekins in the water bath and bake for about 35 minutes; when done the center should still jiggle slightly. Remove the pan from the oven and let the ramekins cool in the water for 10 minutes. Then pop them in the fridge to chill for at least 2 hours.

For the pistachio biscotti, preheat the oven to 350°F. In an electric mixer, beat the butter until light and fluffy. With the mixer running, gradually add the eggs, sugar, and vanilla; mix until creamed. Add the flour, baking powder, and salt. Mix the dough until smooth. Using a wooden spoon, mix in the pistachios until evenly distributed.

Put the dough on a lightly floured surface and cut in half. Roll each half into a log, each 12 inches long by 1 inch high. Place the logs on an ungreased cookie sheet and bake for 35 minutes or until the bottoms are lightly brown. Let the logs cool for 5 minutes and then place on a cutting board. Slice each log on a diagonal into twelve 1-inch-thick pieces. Put the cookies back on the cookie sheet and bake 5 minutes. Turn the cookies over and bake the other side for another 5 minutes. Serve the Espresso Pots de Crème with the cookies on the side for dipping.

Triple Chocolate Threat

 **1½ hours**

This indispensable chocolate cake is perfect for every birthday.

Serves 8 to 12

Chocolate Cake

2½ cups cake flour

1½ teaspoons baking soda

1 teaspoon salt

¾ cup (1½ sticks) unsalted butter, at room temperature

2 cups sugar

3 (1-ounce) squares unsweetened chocolate, melted and cooled

2 eggs

1 teaspoon vanilla extract

1½ cups ice water

Chocolate Chip Frosting

3 cups confectioners' sugar

7 tablespoons hot water

4 (1-ounce) squares unsweetened chocolate, melted and cooled

2 teaspoons vanilla extract

½ cup (1 stick) unsalted butter, at room temperature

¼ cup mini chocolate chips

Preheat the oven to 350°F. Coat two 9-inch round cake pans, including the sides, with nonstick cooking spray. Cut 2 circles of parchment paper to fit the pan bottoms and place them inside the pans; then spray the paper for added nonstick insurance. Set the pans aside.

In a large bowl, sift together the flour, baking soda, and salt; set aside. In the bowl of an electric mixer, cream the butter and sugar until light and fluffy. Add the cooled chocolate and beat for 3 minutes to incorporate. Beat in the eggs one at a time; add the vanilla until well blended. Scrape down the sides of the bowl and beat for another 3 minutes. Gradually mix in the dry ingredients in 3 batches, alternating with the ice water. Beat for 1 minute after each addition to incorporate the ingredients and strengthen the cake's structure. Mix until the batter is smooth.

Pour the batter into the prepared pans and smooth the surface with a spatula; the pans should be two-thirds full. Place the pans on the middle rack of the oven and bake for 30 to 35 minutes, or until a toothpick inserted in the center comes out clean and the cake springs back when touched. Cool the cake in the pans until completely cool, and I mean completely cool. Otherwise you run the risk of these extremely light cakes breaking apart when you take them out. Once cool, turn them out from the pans and remove the parchment paper. Next prepare the frosting.

In the bowl of an electric mixer, dissolve the confectioners' sugar and water at low speed. Add the cooled chocolate and vanilla. Mix until everything is completely incorporated. With the mixer still running, add the butter 1 tablespoon at a time. Using a spatula, fold in the chocolate chips.

With a metal spatula, spread about ½ cup frosting on top of one of the cakes. Carefully place the other layer on top. Frost the top and sides of the cake thoroughly. Refrigerate the cake for 45 minutes before decorating or cutting.

Blackberry and Rosemary Crumble

 1½ **hours**

The rosemary adds a sophisticated taste to this old favorite. It's great in the summertime when black-berries are at their peak.

Serves 8

Crumble

½ cup (1 stick) unsalted butter, at room temperature
1½ cups sugar
1 cup all-purpose flour
Needles from 2 rosemary sprigs

Filling

2 quarts fresh blackberries
½ cup sugar
¼ cup cornstarch
Juice of 1 lemon

To make the crumble topping, mash together the butter, sugar, flour, and rosemary in a large bowl. The best way to do this is with your hands.

In a large bowl, mix the blackberries, sugar, cornstarch, and lemon juice together. Pour the blackberry filling into a 9 × 13-inch glass baking pan; even it out with a spatula. Crumble the topping over the blackberry mixture. Bake for 1 hour on a nonstick cookie sheet (to catch any overflow) until the topping is brown and the fruit is bubbly. Serve the crumble with vanilla ice cream. Make sure the crumble is still a little warm so the ice cream will melt.

Roasted Pineapple with Rum-Vanilla Sauce and Coconut

 **45 minutes**

An elegant and easy dessert that you can bang out in under an hour.

Serves 6

½ cup sugar
2 tablespoons cornstarch
1 teaspoon salt
1½ cups hot water
½ cup white rum
½ vanilla bean, scraped
1 pineapple
½ cup shredded coconut, toasted (see page 88)
1 pint rum raisin ice cream

Preheat the oven to 400°F. In a pot, stir together the sugar, cornstarch, and salt. Add the hot water slowly, whisking constantly. Place the pot over high heat and bring the mixture to a simmer while continuing to whisk. Turn off the heat once the sauce has thickened, 3 to 5 minutes. Add the rum and the vanilla scrapings; stir to incorporate.

Cut the top and bottom off the pineapple with a large sharp knife. Stand the pineapple up on the counter and slice off the rind from top to bottom; then cut it into thirds lengthwise. Cut the wedges in half the short way so you have six thick chunks; remove the cores. Put the pineapple wedges on a non-stick cookie sheet and ladle them with half of the rum sauce. Bake for 30 minutes; then switch the oven to broil and cook until the pineapple is caramelized, 10 to 15 minutes. Serve a hunk of pineapple covered with remaining rum sauce, toasted coconut, and 2 scoops of ice cream.

Spiced Poached Quince

 **1 hour**

Quince is an ancient Roman fruit that looks like a cross between a pear and an apple. It has an amazing aroma when poached.

Serves 8

4 cups water

2 cups sugar

2 cinnamon sticks

1 teaspoon ground cardamom

1 teaspoon allspice

5 whole cloves

2 whole star anise

1 teaspoon fennel seed

1-inch piece fresh ginger, whacked open with the flat side of a knife

1 lemon, halved

1 orange, halved

4 quinces, about 3 pounds, peeled, cored, and halved lengthwise

In a large pot, combine all the ingredients. Bring to a simmer over high heat, stirring several times to dissolve the sugar. Cut a circle of parchment paper just slightly bigger than the opening of your pot. Place the piece of parchment paper on top of the simmering quinces and a small plate on top of the paper to keep the quinces submerged in the syrup. Adjust the heat to keep the quinces simmering but not boiling hard. Simmer for 40 minutes or until the quince halves are easily pierced with a paring knife, but not falling apart. Strain the syrup. Serve the quince halves, warm or at room temperature, in a shallow bowl with some syrup.

Apple Tarte Tatin with Red Wine Caramel and Fresh Thyme

 **1¼ hours**

The red wine caramel adds a sexy complexity to this classic French staple and the fresh thyme gives it a sweet, earthy depth.

Serves 8 to 10

4 tablespoons (½ stick) unsalted butter

1 cup sugar

¼ cup heavy cream

1 cup red wine

½ vanilla bean, split and scraped

1 teaspoon freshly squeezed lemon juice

7 Granny Smith apples, peeled, halved, and cored

2 sheets puff pastry, 1 box, about 1 pound

Leaves from 2 fresh thyme sprigs, for garnish

Preheat the oven to 350°F. Place the butter and sugar in a small pot and cook, stirring constantly, over medium heat until the sugar has melted and caramelized, about 8 minutes. Remove the pot from the burner and add the cream. It will bubble and spit, so be careful. When the sauce has calmed down, return to the flame and add the wine slowly while continually stirring. Add the vanilla scrapings and lemon juice.

Add half the red wine caramel sauce to a 10-inch cast-iron or regular ovenproof skillet. Place the apple halves, cut side up, making sure the apples are snug. Cover the top of the pan completely with the puff pastry by overlapping the two sheets. Snip off the extra dough with scissors to create a circle that just fits inside the pan. Bake for 30 minutes, or until the puff pastry has risen and is golden brown.

Let the tarte rest in the pan for 15 minutes; then place your serving platter on top of the pan, and carefully flip it over. Lift the pan away from the tarte; the beautiful apples will now be on top. Decorate the dessert plates with the remaining sauce, add a slice of the tarte, and garnish with the thyme.

Cinnamon Swirl Pound Cake with Almonds

 **1¾ hours**

You will need a nonstick Bundt pan to make this awesome cake. Store it in an airtight container and you can snack on it for a week.

Serves 12

1 pound (4 sticks) unsalted butter, at room temperature
2 cups sugar
6 eggs, lightly beaten
2 teaspoons vanilla extract
1¼ cups sour cream
4½ cups all-purpose flour
2 cups brown sugar, packed
2 teaspoons ground cinnamon
½ cup blanched almonds, toasted (see page 206)

Spray a Bundt pan with nonstick spray. Preheat the oven to 350°F. In an electric mixer, cream the butter and sugar together until light and fluffy. With the mixer on low, slowly add the eggs until incorporated. Beat in the vanilla and 1 cup of the sour cream. Add the flour gradually and mix until a smooth batter is formed.

In a bowl, mix together the brown sugar, cinnamon, and remaining ¼ cup sour cream. Scatter the toasted almonds in the bottom of the Bundt pan. Pour half of the cake batter over the almonds, then spread the brown sugar mixture evenly on top. Carefully cover with the rest of the cake batter. Insert a table knife or spoon into the pan and swirl the brown sugar mixture into the batter. Be careful not to disturb the almonds or touch the bottom of the pan. Bake for 1 hour or until a wooden toothpick comes out clean when inserted in the center of the cake.

Blue Cheese Soufflé with Chamomile-Fig Compote

 **1 hour**

Photo on page 291

Cheese for dessert is very European and a nice change from an overly sweet indulgence. This savory dessert puffs up so high it's gorgeous; make sure folks are around when you take it out of the oven. An after-dinner experience.

Serves 4

Blue Cheese Soufflé

3 tablespoons unsalted butter, softened, plus
   more for greasing the ramekins

¼ cup sugar, plus more for the ramekins

3 tablespoons flour

1 cup milk, warmed

5 eggs, separated

Pinch of salt

Ground white pepper

Pinch of nutmeg

1 cup crumbled blue cheese

Pinch of cream of tartar

Chamomile-Fig Compote

1 cup sugar

1½ cups water

1 teaspoon freshly squeezed lemon juice

1 chamomile tea bag

12 dried figs, halved

Preheat the oven to 350°F. Prepare four 8-ounce ramekins by greasing them with softened butter and then coating them with sugar, tapping out any excess.

Make a thick béchamel sauce base by melting the 3 tablespoons of butter over low-medium heat in a thick-bottomed pot. Just as the foam subsides, add the flour, stirring constantly with a whisk to prevent lumps. Cook for 2 to 3 minutes to coat the flour with fat and remove the starchy taste; do not allow the roux to brown. Add the warm milk to the mixture and continue to whisk until smooth and thick. Remove from the heat. Beat in the egg yolks one at a time. Season with salt, pepper, and nutmeg. Stir in the cheese until incorporated evenly. Chill the mixture while whipping the egg whites.

In a separate clean bowl beat the egg whites and cream of tartar just until soft peaks form. Fold one third of the beaten whites into the béchamel mixture to lighten it. Then gently fold in the rest. Pour the batter into the prepared ramekins and place on a cookie sheet. Bake on the middle rack for about 25 minutes. The soufflé is done when it has puffed over the rim, the outside is golden, and the center jiggles slightly.

While the soufflés are baking, make the compote. Combine the sugar, water, lemon juice, and chamomile in a pot. Place over medium heat and bring to a boil; cook and stir for 5 minutes. Remove the tea bag and add the dried figs; bring back to a boil and cook for 10 minutes. Crack open the top of the soufflés and pour the compote inside, and serve immediately.

Cheesecake

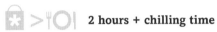 **2 hours + chilling time**

There are no cracks in this New York cheesecake. A water bath is key for gentle heat during the baking process.

Serves 8

Crust

2 cups finely ground graham crackers (about 30 squares)

½ teaspoon ground cinnamon

½ cup (1 stick) unsalted butter, melted

Filling

1 pound cream cheese (2 8-ounce blocks), softened

1 cup sugar

3 eggs

1 teaspoon vanilla extract

Zest of 1 lemon, finely grated

1 pint sour cream

To prepare the crumb crust: In a mixing bowl, combine the crust ingredients with a fork until evenly moistened. Lightly coat the bottom and sides of an 8-inch springform pan with nonstick cooking spray. Firmly press the crumb mixture over the bottom and 1 inch up the sides on the pan using your fingers or the smooth bottom of a glass. Refrigerate the crust while preparing the filling.

To prepare the filling: In a large bowl, beat the cream cheese on low speed for 1 minute just until smooth and free of any lumps. Gradually add the sugar and beat until creamy, 1 to 2 minutes. Periodically scrape down the sides of the bowl and the beaters. Add the eggs, one at a time, and continue to beat slowly until combined. Stir in the vanilla and lemon zest; then blend in the sour cream. The batter should be well mixed but not overbeaten. Pour the filling into the crust-lined pan and smooth the top with a spatula.

Preheat the oven to 325°F. Set the cheesecake pan on a large piece of aluminum foil and fold up the sides around the pan. Carefully set the cake pan in a larger roasting pan. Pour boiling water into the roasting pan until the water is about halfway up the sides of the cheesecake pan; the foil will keep the water from seeping into the cheesecake. Bake for 45 minutes. The cheesecake should still jiggle (it will firm up after chilling), so be careful not to overcook. Let cool in the pan for 30 minutes. Chill in the refrigerator, loosely covered, for at least 4 hours. Loosen the cheesecake from the sides of the pan by running a thin metal spatula around the inside rim. Unmold and transfer to a cake plate. Slice the cheesecake with a thin, nonserrated knife that has been dipped in hot water. Wipe dry after each cut.

Mango, Lime, and Chile Granita

 30 minutes + chilling time

The flavors of mango, lime, and chile are inspired by Mexican street food. Granitas can be made a day or two before serving. Granitas are just as satisfying as ice cream, and you don't need a machine. The flavors are limited only by your imagination.

Serves 8

2 cups water
2 cups sugar
4 limes, zested and juiced
2 pounds mangoes, peeled and cut into chunks
1 tablespoon chile powder

In a large pot over medium heat, combine the water and sugar. Cook and stir until the sugar has dissolved and the syrup looks clear, about 5 minutes. Remove from the heat and cool the syrup by pouring it into a bowl and putting it into the refrigerator or over an ice bath.

Put the sugar syrup, lime zest, lime juice, and mango chunks into a blender. Puree until smooth. Pour the mango mixture into a shallow baking pan and freeze for 1 hour. Using a fork or a couple of chopsticks, break up all the ice crystals on the bottom and sides of the pan. This incorporates air so the final product literally melts in your mouth. Freeze for 3 to 4 hours, until the mixture has reached a frozen granular consistency. You can serve it two ways: Either rake the granita with the tines of a fork for a snow-cone-like product or run an ice-cream scooper down the length for a smooth Italian-ice-like result. Spoon it into a wine or martini glass and lightly sprinkle with the chile powder.

Green Apple Granita

 30 minutes + chilling time

Serves 8

1 cup water
2 cups sugar
Juice of 3 limes
5 Granny Smith apples, about 2 pounds, peeled, cored, and cut into medium dice
½ cup apple liqueur, such as Apple Pucker

In a large pot over medium heat, combine the water and sugar. Cook and stir until the sugar has dissolved and the syrup looks clear, about 5 minutes. Remove from the heat and cool the syrup by pouring it into a bowl and putting it into the refrigerator or over an ice bath.

Put the lime juice into a large bowl. Add the apples to the lime juice, and toss as you go so they don't turn brown. Put the apples and lime juice, sugar syrup, and apple liqueur in a blender; puree until completely smooth. Pour the apple mixture into a shallow baking pan and freeze for 1 hour. Using a fork or a couple of chopsticks, break up all the ice crystals on the bottom and sides of the pan. This incorporates air so the final product literally melts in your mouth. Freeze for 3 to 4 hours, until the mixture has reached a frozen granular consistency. You can serve it two ways: Either rake the granita with the tines of a fork for a snow-cone-like product or run an ice-cream scooper down the length for a smooth Italian-ice-like result. Spoon it into a wine or martini glass.

Lemon Vodka Granita

 30 minutes + chilling time

Serves 8

4 cups water
2 cups sugar
Zest of 3 lemons, finely grated
1 cup freshly squeezed lemon juice, about 5 lemons
1 cup citrus-flavored vodka

In a large pot over medium heat, combine the water and sugar. Cook and stir until the sugar has dissolved and the syrup looks clear, about 5 minutes. Remove from the heat and cool the syrup by pouring it into a bowl and putting it into the refrigerator or over an ice bath. Add the lemon zest and lemon juice; stir to combine. Mix in the lemon vodka.

Pour the lemon mixture into a shallow baking pan and freeze for 1 hour. Using a fork or a couple of chopsticks, break up all the ice crystals on the bottom and sides of the pan. This incorporates air so the final product literally melts in your mouth. Freeze for 3 to 4 hours, until the mixture has reached a frozen granular consistency. You can serve it two ways: Either rake the granita with the tines of a fork for a snow-cone-like product or run an ice-cream scooper down the length for a smooth Italian-ice-like result. Spoon it into a wine or martini glass.

Roasted Apricots with Cherries and Pine Nuts

 **40 minutes**

A contemporary stripped-down fruit dessert that is so unbelievably good, with very few ingredients.

Serves 4 to 8

2 cups water
2½ cups sugar
50 cherries, about ¾ pound or 2 generous cups
1 teaspoon vanilla extract
½ lemon, zest and juice
½ cup coarsely ground pine nuts plus a tablespoon of whole nuts
12 apricots, halved and pitted

In a medium pot, combine the water and 2 cups of the sugar. Cook and stir over medium heat until the sugar has dissolved. Turn the heat up to high and add the cherries, vanilla, lemon zest, and lemon juice. Bring to a boil and cook for 20 minutes.

While the cherries are simmering, turn the oven on to broil. Mix the remaining ½ cup of sugar with the pine nuts and pour onto a plate. Dip the apricot halves cut side down into the sugar-nut mixture. Place the apricots on 2 nonstick cookie sheets, dipped side up. Broil for 5 minutes, until the sugar has caramelized. To serve, put 3 apricot halves on each plate and pour the cherry sauce over. Serve warm or at room temperature.

Index

Note: Pages in *italics* refer to photographs.

The following groovy stores lent me props for photography—check them out.

Moss
146-150 Greene Street
New York, NY 10012
(866) 888-6677
www.Mossonline.com

Troy
138 Greene Street
New York, NY 10012
(212) 941-4777
www.troysoho.com

Broadway Panhandler
477 Broome Street
New York, NY 10013
(866) COOKWARE
www.broadwaypanhandler.com

Tarzian Houseware
194 Seventh Avenue
Brooklyn, NY 11215
(718) 788-4213

Takashimaya
693 Fifth Avenue
New York, NY 10022
(212) 350-0100

Williams-Sonoma
Locations nationwide
(877) 812-6235
www.willamssonoma.com

Pottery Barn
Locations nationwide
(888) 779-5176
www.potterybarn.com